GENUINE DIALOGUE *and* REAL PARTNERSHIP:

GENUINE DIALOGUE *and* REAL PARTNERSHIP:

FOUNDATIONS OF TRUE COMMUNITY

Maurice Friedman

in association with

David Damico

Order this book online at www.trafford.com
or email orders@trafford.com

Most Trafford titles are also available at major online book retailers.

Printed in the United States of America.

ISBN: 978-1-4269-5342-2 (sc)
ISBN: 978-1-4269-5756-7 (hc)
ISBN: 978-1-4269-5343-9 (e)

Library of Congress Control Number: 2011902029

Trafford rev. 03/23/2011

 www.trafford.com

North America & international
toll-free: 1 888 232 4444 (USA & Canada)
phone: 250 383 6864 ♦ fax: 812 355 4082

"Only persons who are capable of truly saying *Thou* to one another can truly say *We* with one another."

- Martin Buber

"We expect a theophany of which we know nothing but the place, and the place is called community."

- Martin Buber

"Whenever persons meet in a spirit of common concern, ready to encounter each other through and beyond their differences, the reality of genuine community can come to being."

- Maurice Friedman

CONTENTS

PART THREE – PERSONAL UNIQUENESS, NON-VIOLENCE, AND RELIGIOUS PLURALISM

Preface

"All men desire peace, yet few desire the things that make for peace," wrote Thomas a Kempis, author of the medieval devotional classic *Imitatio Christi*. The same might be said in regard to community: All persons desire community, yet few desire the things that make for true community. We can put together á Kempis' statement and my own if we turn to the Hebrew word for peace, *shalom*; for *shalom* is nothing other than the never completed task of building true community. Community is the seeking need of our age. Though few of us may actively desire what makes for genuine community, we are all one way or another on the road to true community. In our age of multiethnic, multicultural, multireligious, and multinational diversity, this is what humanity is necessarily concerned with.. By the most varied paths and the most variegated methods we are all working to transform the Babel of voices into a great antiphonal chorus. If this chorus is to be achieved, no voice can rightly drown out another since all voices contribute to the cacophonic yet harmonious whole.

Once when I was teaching at the New School for Social Research in New York City, a woman came up to me after my lecture and asked me whether I would come for dinner to her home in City Island to meet with her and a group of friends to discuss their idea of going West to found a homesteading community. I accepted her invitation and enjoyed a very pleasant dinner and conversation with the small group of five or six who wished to form this community. After dinner I asked each of them what their motivation was for starting this community. Every one of the five answered without exception that it was to give them the opportunity to pursue their individual intellectual and artistic goals. Not one of them showed any concern for the group as a group. I told them they reminded me of the ill-fated nineteenth century Brooks Farm experiment of Bronson Alcott, Margaret Fuller, Hawthorne, and other "transcendentalists" and suggested that they would fail too and for the same reason. Like the group of would-be homesteaders, all the members of Brook Farm were only interested in finding outlets for their creativity and not in building a community together

Only recently a member of the small commune that Jerry Brown, former Governor of California, has established in Oakland reported his first conversation with Jerry Brown: "So I hear you are a recovering drug addict," said the former governor. "So I hear you are a recovering politician!" retorted the man, whom Brown forthwith took into his tiny commune. Apolitician like Jerry Brown "recovering" and forming a commune is a correction of what the great contemporary Jewish philosophe Martin Bubercalls the domination of the "political principle" over the "social principle" of fellowship and spontaneity. After I had added this paragraph to the Preface of this book, Jerry Brown called me up and arranged to interview me on his radio program "We the People" concerning Buber's view of community! This seemed to me a strtiking confirmation of this movement from the political to the social. My own search for community has been integrally connected with my life's work, beginning with my years as a student at Harvard and continuing to the present day so I was gladdened both by what Martin Buber wrote and by Jerry Brown's positive interest in it.

True community is difficult to define. What makes some communities thrive and others fall by the wayside? Can a community be tailor-made to the individual interests and needs of its members? Is community simply a question of group feeling? Can it be aimed at directly and erected by some sort of social engineering, such as Walden Two--the commune in Virginia built on the principles of B.F. Skinner's utopia?]

I believe that the warp of community is the actual relationships that exist among its members and the woof the structures that facilitate or obstruct these relationships. Without genuine relationships there can be no true community. That is why this book does not start with a description of "True Community" as a finished Utopian reality but with an in depth plumbing of the types of relationships and structures that make real community possible.

True community is not an ideal or a specific goal. It is a direction of movement. Or rather it is a twofold direction of movement -- a movement within each particular structure of family, community, and society to discover the maximum possibilities of the confirmation of individuals as true others within that structure, and a movement from structure to structure toward more genuine community.

The aim of this book is not modest. It proposes nothing less than to do away with the old and tired polarities of individual versus society, individualism versus collectivism, competition versus cooperation, free enterprise versus socialism, capitalism versus communism, freedom versus social welfare. In the place of all these it puts forward the confirmation of otherness as the *only* meaningful direction of movement for friendship, marriage, family, community, and society within a democracy. If the confirmation of otherness were sufficiently extended and deepened, it might no longer be a contradiction in terms to speak of a "caring society."

A large number of people have helped me in my attempt to make this book "reader friendly": my former wife Eugenia Friedman, my wife Aleene Friedman, Ph.D., my friends Royal Alsup, Ph.D., Kathy Rose, Ph.D., Louise Goodman, Ph.D., and Richard Farson, Ph.D., the former *Los Angeles Times* editor Noel Greenwood, Leslie Berman, Senior Editor of Psychology for Jossey-Bass publishers, and above all my friend and former student David Damico who has served as a catalytic agent to bring me to a final radical revision of this book. Over more than eight years David Damico has worked with me, selflessly devoting an amazing amount of his time and energy to this project. My thanks to all these friends and helpers is accompanied by the hope that we have succeeded in making *Genuine Dialogue and Real Partnership—Foundations of True Community* accessible to most readers.

Maurice Friedman
Solana Beach, California 2011

INTRODUCTION

Seeking True Community

Between following a script and aimless wandering

There is no shortage of things to turn to in our western culture that promise opportunity, wealth, happiness, and self-fulfillment at almost every turn. We are a culture with a dizzying need to consume those things that offer to make us feel less alone. At the same time, we have confused notions of what it means to be a "healthy," functional adult. We must need others but not be too dependent, we should be generous but not gullible, we must not exclude others unlike ourselves but find our lives compartmentalized so that we mostly interact with people of our educational, social or religious classes. We have a sense of what it means to be an individual, as in "our own person," and describe ourselves to others by virtue of our achievements, pursuits and frustrations. We also have life–long experiences of being affiliated with institutions both-secular and religious.

All through life we make and remake ourselves. Some people do this with a sense of order, as though following a well-constructed outline or script. There are also people who seem to wander aimlessly, always searching, never quite finding peace or happiness.

Near the beginning of my search for a deeper meaning to life, I met Abraham Joshua Heschel and Martin Buber and discovered the importance of bringing my deepest longings and inmost searching needs into focus. This has been a life-long process, and not without periods of loneliness and isolation. Yet my life's direction has been guided by much of what I learned from these two great men.

My Personal Struggle With Decision and Indecision

I became a conscientious objector during World War II. By doing so, I rejected the script my family, friends and country would have had me follow. The decision to become a conscientious objector was not rebellious on my part; the decision of whether or not to join the war was not an opportunity to become my own person at the expense of patriotism, loyalty to family or hatred for Fascism. I became a conscientious objector because I believed (and still do) from the deepest part of my being that war could not be a means to a good end. The experience of choosing to be a conscientious objector, and living with that choice for the rest of my life, punctuates my purpose for writing this book. Had I no sense of belonging to society or caring about the suffering of others who were being oppressed, the decision to become a conscientious objector would have been an easy one. In fact, it was probably the most difficult and certainly the most anguished decisions I ever made.

In 1946 I left Civilian Public Service Camp and, like many other young men my age, tried to make a postwar life for myself. This coincided with my meeting with the great Jewish philosopher and mystic Abraham Joshua Heschel. Professor Heschel arranged for me to spend a Shabbat weekend at the home of a Williamsburg, Brooklyn Hasid. At one time during that weekend I stood from ten till two in the morning in a tiny room (*shtuebl*) packed with over a hundred disciples of the Satmor Rebbe, good-naturedly fighting and shoving for the *shirayim,* food that the Rebbe gives from his thirteen-course meal. I was deeply impressed, particularly at one point when, after wishing the Rebbe would pass me a drumstick and then thinking that, dressed as I was, I was the last person he would thus honor, some one handed me a drumstick and said, "The Rebbe sent this for you!" This experience was quite foreign to the individualized consciousness of a "modern Jew" such as myself, however, for there was no way in which I could make my own the sense of a childlike devotion of the Hasidim to the Rebbe.

When I next visited Williamsburg to witness the dancing on Simhas Torah, the feast of the celebration of the giving of the Torah, I naively went with a non-Jewish friend to inquire as to the time of the services of the Klausenberger Rebbe.. I was met by a young man with a bright red beard who asked me in a very confrontational tone, "Are you a Jew?" "Yes," I replied. "Do you speak Yiddish?" "No," I said. "You are a Jew and you don't speak Yiddish!" His contempt for me was obvious. He then turned to my friend whose bow tie and cap marked him as a smart Greenwich Villager, and exclaimed indignantly as though my friend were less than human, "And you brought him into the Synagogue!" My friend shrank out the door, and I began to wonder how I could experience such a sense of genuine community in my first foray with Hasidism only to encounter a hatred fueled by fear of those outside the group when meeting a real live Hasid other than Heschel himself, who did not live in a Hasidic community.

To What Should We Turn?

Abraham Heschel said to me that everyone has something that he turns to in his or her life, and he believed that for me it was Hasidism. Heschel was right in that Hasidism provided a touchstone for me, not as a dogma or systematic teaching but in the tales of the Hasidim to which I have turned again and again in the years that followed. To be sure, I was not able to join what seemed to me the closed communities of contemporary Hasidim. Nonetheless, I found in traditional Hasidism, in so far as I could grasp it from the tales and teaching and from my friendship with Heschel, basic attitudes that lie at the heart of all genuine community: I have tried to live by these attitudes for more than fifty years by relating to others (as teacher, counselor, therapist, mentor, and friend) with a spirit of openness and inclusion.

Although I became a mystic during my years in Civilian Public Service and my sole concern during that time was my relationship to God, I felt strongly even then that I should not let it cut me off from the sufferings of others. In Dostoevsly/s great novel *The Brothers Karamazov* I cherished Father Zossima's mysticism of reciprocity and active love. Similarly, in the parable of the nineteenth century Hindu saint Sri Ramakrishna, I preferred the savior who comes back from the garden to help others to the saints who go down into the garden and stay there. and leave the world behind.

In the course of a long life I have learned a few things that are helpful for those who want true community. One is that it is not enough simply to defend one's convictions in words. One must live them. As David Damico has pointed out from his extensive experience, the most rigidly defensive posture is often found in the most orthodox of individuals and institutions. The spirit of community cannot be safeguarded by dogma or protected by doctrine. No one can lay claim to the spirit of community because it does not exist in the same way a piece of land exists. It arises in those individuals and communities whose loyalty to life overcomes their compulsion to self-protect.

This leads in turn to moving in the direction of more equitable, inclusive communities. and confronting institutional injustice The search for true community often begins when we discover that institutional communities do not act according to their own ideals. For many as a result, moving in the direction of true community begins with a social protest movement, such as the civil rights movement, the women's movement, the gay rights movement. The goal of any movement must be first of all to formulate a rationale for the restoration of inclusion and to demonstrate inclusion in simple acts (such as allowing a gay boy scout to participate with his peers.)

We must above all make room for the seeking needs of others. Institutional communities are notorious for marginalizing those within their ranks who don't conforms to their ideals and/or values. So many of us in search of true community are really hoping to find a more tolerant, accepting institution. Sadly, many stay attached to institutions where in order to achieve status and esteem of peers they must pretend to be something they are not and hide what they really are.

We should participate in moments and events of relationship where we will be forced to face and solve seemingly insoluble problems. How often do we take the easy way by simply eliminating the complications without understanding the complexities that go with relating to others who challenge, confront, and unnerve us.

Most important of all, we must move from feelings of mistrust that inhibit our relating to others. How often do we consider helping others only to reject the idea when we fear we will be taken advantage of. Defining true community, therefore,, has less to do with adopting a philosophy of life than with becoming less sedentary in our ways and responding to the world around us. Dialogue, reciprocity, and love are to real partnership what yoga is to the contemplative mystic. –a daily exercize of mind, body, and spirit in moving to greater awareness. The limit of dialogue is the limit of awareness, Martin Buber has said. We must learn to connect our intentions with our attitudes, with our actions, with our interactions, and with our decisions—in that order. Life is like a knife's edge said one Hasidic *zaddik*, or leader. We must learn to balance and be in relation to the blade or else be cut in half

Being in true community also means we must be true as members of institutional communities. Real partnership means living on what Martin Buber calls "the narrow ridge." Each of us is called to be our best, most active , most loving self. It is not enough to pledge allegiance to principles of love and goodwill to others only to ignore opportunities to extend love and good will in our daily encounter with our fellows. That means, certainly, we must overcome the inertia that leads us to do nothing in the face of opportunities to act.

We make a mistake when we associate a spirit of true community with an institution, secular or religious to the extent that we feel that we can only participate in true community as long as we are members of that institution. We also often ignore the fact that institutions can make demands on us in the name of community that work against the kinds of attitudes that keep a spirit of true community alive.

Martin Buber's book *The Legend of the Baal-Shem*, gave me my first image of active love and fervent devotion in a context of service to others. Hasidism (founded by the Baal-Shem) spoke to me in compelling accents of wholehearted service to God that did not mean turning away from my fellows and from the world. A new image of human spirituality offered itself to me. I realized that fulfillment and redemption take place through the dedication that one brings to one's every act.

Another wise zaddik once said that the way of like is like a knife's edge. There is an abyss on either side, and the way of life lies in between. This tale expresses beautifully the "narrow ridge" that was so central to Buber and that became central to me. I have learned that the spirit of genuine community and partnership exists when two or more people meet on the narrow ridge between institutional fundamentalism and reckless individualism.

PART ONE

CREATING REAL PARTNEERSHIPS
THROUGH GENUINE DIALOGUE

CHAPTER 1

The Life of Community Needs Genuine Dialogue

Martin Buber's Life of Dialogue & the Interhuman

My encounter with Martin Buber, first in his classic *I and Thou* and his other books and later through my many meetings with him by letter and in person, was a momentous turning point in my life. I came to understand that Buber's life of dialogue was a foundation that I was missing in the institutional communities I had previously encountered.. I realized that socialism looked to an external or outer community, and mysticism to an inward one, but neither glimpsed the reality of the "interhuman"--what takes place between one person and another.

Among the members of every real group there exists an interhuman exchange that Buber saw as the true touchstone for genuine dialogue. I am deeply convinced that this is the foundation stone of real partnership and real community. In the life of dialogue real partnership takes place when we muster up the courage to respond to the people (our family, our neighbors, our co-workers, and our friends) and situations in which we are set by our life circumstances.. If the life of dialogue ceases to exist and the spirit of genuine community dies, we are left with an institutional shell that may function well but will leave those in search of real partnership wanting more.

Dialogue is More Than Having Things in Common

It is an illusion to think that real partnership can be achieved when two people or groups of people are focused on getting their needs met, even if in the interest of self-discovery, personal wholeness or spiritual growth. Institutional community must call upon its members for their gifts, talents and contributions in order to survive. But if members of institutions are going to form real and lasting partnerships with one another, they must be in genuine dialogue. How often have we contributed our time, talents and resources to communities where we then realized that our importance was largely rooted in the role or duty we performed? A real partnership must go beyond one person's laying claim to another's abilities for the sake of the community.

Making Real the Life of Dialogue

Can community exist without making the life of dialogue a reality? If community exists on a "narrow ridge, " as we shall suggest, what's to keep us all from falling off into the abysses of disappointment, cynicism or mistrust? The answer is a difficult one. We must begin by recognizing that perfect communities where everyone does the right thing all of the time do not exist. Mistrust is a result of falling out of relationship. Forgiveness is the steep climb back to the life of dialogue. We are constantly falling and climbing, renewed by the life of dialogue that calls us to respond anew. We overcome mistrust when we reach out toward new experiences and deeper relationships with others in spite of past failures to meet and connect.

Several years ago I received a call from Carl, a high school friend who had got hold of my book *The Confirmation of Otherness: In Family, Community, and Society.* "With your strong belief in community, I am hoping that you would be willing to come out to the Midwest and join me in an intentional community that I am founding." For me, this was an impossible request since I was firmly planted in San Diego.

A few years later, I received another call from Carl asking again for a meeting. I agreed this time hoping there might be some way I could help him with his search for community. Carl surprised me when he said over the phone, "I want you to sign a document witnessing that you will take this meeting wholly seriously."

"I can't do that, Carl," I replied, "it goes against all my concern for spontaneity in genuine dialogue."

Carl's mistrust left me feeling distinctly uneasy because he had an agenda that did not leave room for my genuine contribution. His inability to let me reach out to him in a real response destroyed all possible spontaneity and with it the life of dialogue. While I can sympathize with his mistrust as well as identify with his desire to create a "safe" community, I cannot support an approach that leads right back to the same loneliness.

Reluctant as we may be to see it, there is a little of Carl in every one of us. We all have enough mistrust that we bring the "answers" with us to new situations usually even before we have heard the questions that that situation confronts us with. Mistrust makes us want to manipulate others to bring them around to our point of view or at least hope, by a winning smile or a charming gesture, to persuade them to come over to our side of the "argument." In fact, there is much that we can learn from Carl in his very fanaticism. While it is important that we acknowledge our mistrust, we must make room for the genuine responses of others in order to engage in the life of dialogue

The Life of Dialogue, the "We" and the "Sphere of the Between"

The life of dialogue means we must at times stretch our trust to its limit. A new situation calls for more trust than a previous one did. Whenever we are outside our comfort zones and attempting to forge new paths in our personal lives, we run a great risk of being disappointed, misled, misunderstood or taken advantage of. This is because we are working hard to stay open-minded. One person said it best when, after being used by one group for her legal expertise she remarked, "I had a feeling from the beginning that I was being invited to join the group because they wanted a free lawyer, but I kept telling myself I was being too quick to judge. I felt I needed to give them the benefit of the doubt. Even after I agreed to provide some limited assistance, I repressed the urge to set clear boundaries for fear of seeming mistrustful." Another friend said, "Maurice, I have been thinking about how hard it is to be in community and not feel sure that I won't be taken advantage of. I don't want to be guarded or unavailable. I like people to feel they can come to me if they need something." I responded by saying, "It's your job to tell people what they can and can't expect from you. You cannot assume that others will know what makes you feel taken advantage of."

On one side of the dialogue there you sit; on the other side sits a potential partner. Each has the responsibility to give of oneself in proportion to his level of trust. Partnership grows out of a trusting (but not overly naïve) give and take. Rebbe Yitzhak Eisik of Zhydatcov said, "The motto of life is give and take. Everyone must be both a giver and a receiver. He who is not both is a barren tree."

The "sphere of the between" is what Martin Buber calls the basic reality of human life. This sphere is somewhat difficult to grasp at first. The "between" is the "we" that enables two friends or lovers to say "I miss us" and even to fight with real caring and anger for the "us" that is neglected or denied. In my experience, when marriages or friendships end, they do so because the reality of "we" has been denied or rejected. One partner is dismissed as an object with fixed properties. "How could I have wasted fifteen years of my life with such a loser?" or "Geoffrey is a wimp!"

When a partnership is alive, each partner knows that the "we" is the heart of what they experience as true friendship and genuine love. When I participate in your life as a true friend, I am not preoccupied with trying to become what I think you want me to be. And you are not an image in my mind that I compare with other images of friendship. I am a friend who meets you in each new situation as myself, caring deeply about a reality that exists between us. This kind of relationship requires each of us to be a real person in our own right. We must be able to meet each other as we know ourselves to be.

The great Jewish sage Hillel, who lived 75 years before Jesus, said "If I am not for myself, who will be for me? And if I am for myself alone, what am I? And if not now, when?" Some people live in the illusion that they are self-sufficient or, worse yet, pursue self-sufficiency with the assumption that it is a cornerstone of maturity. "I don't need anyone and I don't want to need anyone. I can take care of myself."

Imagine being in a partnership with someone who spoke and acted as though they were the center of the universe and everyone else was there to serve their interests and needs. In the end, such a relationship can make us feel invisible, voiceless, used and angry. A student of mine at Sarah Lawrence College once came to a conference in my office and announced, "I am God and you are a thought in my mind." "How would you feel," I countered, "if I said that *I* am God and you are a thought in my mind?" "Just fine," she exclaimed, "because that is the way I want you to think!" While not many people will express their narcissistic notions the way she did, a lot of people *act* as if they were God and everyone else was a thought in their mind though they try to *appear* to be caring and concerned for others.

In an age in which people tend to make everything psychological, it is difficult to understand Buber's sphere of the between. We tend to focus on what happens within the soul of each partner and see the relation between two people as a byproduct of an inner process or reality. In order to understand Buber's sphere of the between and the life of dialogue, a less psychological approach to relationship must be taken. Center stage in Buber's life of dialogue is the sphere of the between, the "I-Thou" relationship. The "within" of each partner is merely the secret accompaniment to the dialogue itself.

This recognition that true community only comes into being when two or more persons come together in real partnership is the heart of Martin Buber's famous distinction between the "I-It" relationship and the "I-Thou" relationship. An "I-It" relation is one in which we relate to the other merely as someone to be known and used.

My friend Carl's meeting with me is an example of an "I-It" relation. The "I-Thou" relationship is one in which we bring ourselves into a direct open, present, and, in important ways, mutual relationship. This is not a moral distinction but a fundamental human one. "I-It" is necessary for our existence, but it does not bring two people to true meeting. The central statement of Buber's classic book *I and Thou* is, "All real living is meeting."

While many people would define dialogue in some ordinary or generic sense as the words used by characters in a play or even the exchange between persons when they bump into one another in everyday life, Buber's dialogue means much more. It means the real meeting between two persons where the invisible yet palpable reality of the "between" comes into being. Thus it is never just the sum of what goes on within each person or even the sum of their feelings and attitudes toward each other. This goes against the popular notion in the current self-help culture today that we can become our "real selves" without having real relationships with others. Actually we only become ourselves in genuine dialogue with others. This means that we come to know ourselves as our uniqueness is made present in partnership with someone who can embrace us in that uniqueness. In this context, we can understand that self-realization is a true by-product of the life of dialogue. Once I sought to become more whole without the life of dialogue. But in the course of years I discovered that as I grew in the courage to respond faithfully to situations, both difficult and ordinary, I became more whole.

Dialogue Is Distancing *and* Relating

If self-realization is the byproduct of genuine dialogue, what then is the goal? The goal is to bridge any distance between us that might prevent us from entering real partnership. Partnership here means inclusion, mutual confirmation and cooperation. Buber helps us understand what it means to bridge distance in his book, *The Knowledge of Man,* "Distancing is the first of the two primary movements that distinguishes the human being from all the other animals, the second being entering into relation."

Distancing underlies both Buber's "I-It" and "I-Thou" relationships; in both distancing is an important movement. However, when distancing becomes a stance as opposed to a movement, the second movement of entering into relation cannot take place and dialogue is blocked. There are many ways to thicken the distance in relation with someone else: observation, analysis, judgment and even desire can block dialogue. Distancing and relating is a continual dynamic — a dance between one pole and the other. When distancing is used as a stance, either for self-protection or a means of avoidance, the dance pauses and a category of thought or an idea or feeling is substituted for the living flow of thoughts, ideas and feelings.

I am called into being by you and you by me. The very essence and meaning of the self is this interrelatedness. In real partnerships, it is important that we set one another at a distance and view each other as independent. This enables us to enter into relationship as individual selves.. It is also important that you embrace me as the unique person that I am. When you confront me in your own uniqueness, the distance between us is bridged. Through this distancing and relating we confirm each other as the unique persons we are. By bridging the distance between us and repeatedly entering into relationship with each other, we cultivate the sphere of the between and strengthen the "we" that Buber describes.

What I am saying here points to a reality that is even more basic than ethics and morality. In *Man's Hope*, Andre Malraux's novel about the Spanish civil war, a scene is described in which two men from opposite sides of the war come around a corner and meet face to face. One of the men is carrying a flame-thrower, the other only a gun. The first man is unable to train the flame-thrower on his enemy while looking in his eyes, and this gives the other man time to shoot him. The paralysis of the flame-thrower has nothing to do with loving one's neighbor or any other moral or altruistic injunction. What happens is simply that looking into the eyes of the other, he recognizes his enemy as a self like himself, someone whose existence as a self is inextricably connected with his own existence as a self. Therefore, he is unable to burn him alive while seeing his eyes seeing him. This story has meaning for us all. Even if you threaten me by your uniqueness, I must find a way to keep you fixed in my gaze until an understanding breaks through.

Dialogue Transcends Conditional Relations

Many of us, unfortunately, have experienced "confirmation" with strings attached. We have been offered a contract that reads: "We will confirm you only if you will conform to our model of the good child, the good citizen, the good soldier." We cannot become ourselves without other people who call us to realize our created uniqueness.

Most of us fall somewhere between feeling we have a right to exist because we are persons and feeling our right to exist must be justified at every moment by producing, accomplishing, or performing. Have you ever been criticized in a way that made you feel that not only what you do but who you are is being attacked? Maybe you have known someone who is driven to perform because they feel they must justify their existence at every turn.

As a teacher and counselor I have many times had to be critical of students and clients. When this happens, I am reminded how important confirmation is. I often think of a Vassar student whom I admired both as a person and as a student. After I had read her term paper, I said to her, "I really feel that this paper needs to be rewritten. You did not flunk, but somehow it just does not hold together." She looked at me as if to ask, "Are you merely saying my *paper* is no good or are you really saying that *I* am no good?" I wanted her to sense that I really cared for her while being truthful about the inadequacy of her work.

Most of us are sensitive to criticism and can feel invalidated by the particular criticisms of significant people like parents, teachers, counselors or employers. The struggle between being confirmed for who we are and knowing there are strings attached can place us in an impossible double bind. We know somewhere in our heart of hearts that it is not we who are being confirmed, but rather the roles that we play to please others. Yet if we try to rebel against this pseudo-confirmation in the interest of a more authentic way of relating, we risk rejection or dismissal. As a result, we thicken the distance between ourselves and others, sometimes not meaning to; closing the door to those who might truly confirm us without strings attached. This paradox is at the heart of the life of dialogue.

A distinction must be made between a basic confirmation that gives us our ticket to exist and the confirmation along the road that has to do with the way in which we exist. Both are important, but the basic confirmation that gives us our ticket to exist helps us open ourselves out to the confirmation along the road that speaks to the directions we choose in life. If we have not experienced basic confirmation, a void is left that all the later confirmation we receive is not likely to fill.

Dialogue is "Inclusion" or "Imagining the Real"

One misleading notion would be to think that I should be so taken with you that I lose my own sense of being grounded in the relationship. One woman said, "Intimacy to me means my husband and I are always of the same mind and wavelength." Buber's inclusion is not synonymous with being symbiotically joined. Inclusion is "imagining the real" which means to experience the other side of the relationship while not losing your own ground in the process.

Imagining what you are perceiving, thinking, feeling, and willing is how I include you genuinely in the life of dialogue. I can be empathetic or intuitive in our relationship, but unless I swing boldly and wholeheartedly in your direction I will not make you fully present to me. Any lesser action on my part will result in my including you in part — keeping you at a distance by way of distraction or disinterest. If you have ever been the object of someone's undivided attention, then you have experienced genuine inclusion in the life of dialogue.

It is in the process of being fully present in partnership to you that I cultivate the life of dialogue. When I see you in your unique and separate way of responding to a situation that is common to us both, I am practicing inclusion.

Inclusion does not ensure that we will succeed. It is tempting for people, like the wife I just described, to orchestrate circumstances so as to demand a particular response from a partner or spouse. This kind of well-meant manipulation would immediately thicken the distance and close the way for an I-Thou relationship to unfold.

17

To cultivate the life of dialogue we must risk disappointment. The courage to respond to the person who has disappointed us at one time in one situation is the challenge we all face when we participate in the life of dialogue.

The Life of Dialogue Leads to the Narrow Ridge of Community

Martin Buber often spoke of walking on the "narrow ridge" between abysses--an image so central to his life and thought that I used it as the title of my one-volume biography of him.[1] One of the many meanings of this metaphor is the difficult path we have to follow if we are to avoid the simple either/ors into which our thinking usually leads us. This is particularly true of the life of dialogue.

We are used to thinking in terms of polarities. The individual versus community, or inner versus outer. But to see only the polar extremes obscures a great deal of human reality. The primary human reality is the life of dialogue that takes place *in* family and *in* community. To view the individual or the community outside the context of the life of dialogue is like trying to draw a map of the world with only the north and south poles as references. For the life of dialogue, the self vs. the world is an abstract notion. The self in the world is the basic reality we all share. While we exist in many and often different modes, sometimes pitted against the world and sometimes part of it, the life of dialogue calls each of us to respond to the unique moment and circumstance in which we find ourselves. To this extent, the life of dialogue strengthens real community that stands on the narrow ridge between a complete withdrawal from the world and a complete surrender to it.

The Life of Dialogue Goes beyond Inner and Outer

Most of us believe we are composed of an inner and an outer dimension. When one person says, I'm an introvert, we immediately know she is probably shy and not very social. When another person describes himself as an extrovert, we imagine he is easy to talk to and self-assured. We might even presume that being one or the other automatically makes life in the world easier or more difficult. In my dialogue with some of my Jungian friends, I have occasionally been shocked to discover both Buber and myself labeled as extroverts, as if the life of dialogue meant turning to the other at the expense of one's own inwardness!

Inner and outer are constructions arising from a human wholeness that precedes them both and gives rise to them. Only the possibility of direct contact between whole human beings gives rise to the sphere of the between. Divisions between inner and outer are useful for a certain ordering of our lives, such as the distinction between what we see, what we dream, what we envision, and what we hallucinate. Yet a true event in our lives is neither inner nor outer but takes up and claims the whole of us. When I give a lecture there is no way I can divide the event into inner feelings and outer impressions. My response to the audience comes from the whole of who I am as I stand in their presence and experience, both psychically and physically, the event.

Only if we can get beyond this deep-seated construct of inner and outer can we understand the sense in which the life of dialogue can alone be fully realized in the sphere of the between. I meet you from my ground and you meet me from yours, and our lives interpenetrate as person meeting person in the life of dialogue.

The Life of Dialogue and Inwardness

You might be thinking that with such a radical shift of emphasis I am doing away with genuine inwardness. In my early years, I tried to become a real person by turning away from others and focusing on my own individuation with the hope of later turning more effectively to others. These inward years were indispensable for me. But to the extent that I aimed at inwardness as my ultimate goal, I was denying myself a part in the life of dialogue.

Some psychologists, like the Jungians, contend that individuation is necessary for the realization of the self and also for meaningful relationships with others. I agree insofar as our relationships are distorted by those projections on to others of unappealing aspects of ourselves that we do not wish to own. But it is precisely through the life of dialogue that we become real persons. One client spent three years working on his ambivalent feelings toward his mother only to come back after meeting a woman he planned to marry with the shocking discovery that at times he felt the same ambivalence with her. He mistakenly thought that by working on himself he would never have another ambivalent relationship. "I thought I dealt with that." was his response to me. "You can't deal with 'it' apart from the person with whom you are relating. Three years ago it was your mother. Now it's your girlfriend."

CHAPTER 2

Real Partnership Requires
Awareness of Oneself and Others

What is the Relationship between the Life of Dialogue and Real Partnership?

The life of dialogue makes real partnership possible. These two are as integral to each other as fingers are to hands. This is true even when real partnerships suffer difficult setbacks. Within the realm of the interhuman, real partnerships are the cornerstones of genuine community. The life of dialogue forms the relational glue that makes it possible for real partnerships to be both cohesive and responsive; introspective and reflective; separate yet connected

The Paradox of Being Separate yet Connected

The fact that we exist with others like ourselves is self-evident. A second fact, more difficult to grasp psychologically, is that we are fundamentally and remarkably unique. When you say "I" to me you imply that you are separate from me. The fact that each of us can say "I" when relating to each other identifies our uniqueness and our singleness. At the same time, the fact that you and I can form a relational identity and refer to ourselves as "we" identifies the degree to which we can connect.

This amazing paradox is illustrated in the marvelous myth that Plato puts into the mouth of Aristophanes in his great dialogue, *The Symposium*. In this myth people are pictured as originally having four arms and four legs and rolling around the world and challenging the gods to combat. Then Zeus cuts them in half--effectively separating them. Immediately each half throws its arms around the other, and they cling together until Zeus separates them again. From that moment they go around the world, each looking for his or her other half. They are not self-sufficient as halves, but neither can they ever become whole again by finding their other halves. This wonderful paradigm of human existence teaches us that we are unique persons, but we are not self-sufficient humans (as nineteenth-century American individualism imagined.)

The paradox is hardly comprehensible. I as "I" am more than a mere confluence of social and psychological forces and influences. If I am going to talk about any sort of personal uniqueness, there has to be that *I* in me that can respond. It's easier to see this personal uniqueness when we think of people like Dr. Martin Luther King and Gandhi who demonstrated a uniqueness beyond the cultures that helped shape them. What's important here is to recognize that each of us responds daily to circumstances that challenge us to respond as unique selves. To the extent that we respond in ways that are culturally appropriate but not particularly unique, we fail to introduce that unique "I" to the world--we do not contribute to the life of dialogue. The essential "I" is not an "essence," like a vein of gold that runs through a mountain waiting to be mined. Though we may view ourselves in large part through our relationships with parents, friends, teachers, and other influential people, we become most truly ourselves by searching for the most genuine response to what calls us.

It would have been easier, in many ways, for me to enlist in the armed forces during World War II. The decision to become a conscientious objector was an unpopular and socially unacceptable one. However, it was my most genuine response. It rubs against the grain of cultural pressure to subjugate one's personal response to a social problem in order to support a larger cause. I am sure there were many black Americans who did not like Martin Luther King Jr.'s disregard for the status quo. Ultimately, it is discomfort with the very paradox of being separate yet connected that makes most people hide their true selves even when they know they are doing injury to themselves and others by forbidding the awakening of that unique response.

Real Partnership Needs A Responding "I"

Dr. Royal Alsup, a marriage and family counselor with a particular interest in Native American Indians, sees real partnerships" as central to the life of the Native American. In this connection he tells of an American Indian woman who was a client of his. This woman had been suffering from anxiety because she had a serious argument with her father who died before she could heal the relationship. She shared a dream she had with Dr. Alsup where she drove into a large parking lot and was greeted by a lot of Indian children laughing and having fun. They brought her close to a river that was swift and had a lot of power. She followed the children into the water where they sank to a deep cave. In that cave she saw her father. She saw that he was doing fine. She also felt a telepathic communication with him that told her he was forgiving her. Then she saw a light that spoke to her saying, "You have been brought here by Thunder beings. Now you will go back because you don't belong here and you will have power and courage." Afterward, she shot through the water and was put back on land on top of a large mountain where a child was hugging her. That's where the dream ended. So did the panic attacks she'd been suffering from for more than eighteen months.

Not everyone has such a dramatic experience when struggling to yield to the awakening of a personal response. Anxiety, depression, guilt, and many other psychological complexes have, at their root, an ailing "I". This was powerfully illustrated in the Novel *Ordinary People* where a young man struggles to keep himself from committing suicide after a boating accident that kills his brother—the family hero. He would almost rather die than betray his dead brother by recalling the true details that led to his death. It's only after he finds the courage to respond to his own guilt for having survived, his fear of his mother's rejection, and his anger at himself over realizing that his own will to survive kept him holding on for dear life while his brother slipped into the storm and drowned, that he is able to emerge from his depression and connect more genuinely with his friends, father, and therapist.

Real Partnership Needs A Trusting We

My wife Aleene is a person who lives in real partnership with others. She is a gifted biofeedback therapist, treating pain and stress. Rather than focusing on the technicalities of biofeedback machines, Aleene emphasizes the "healing partnership." Jane and Harold came to Aleene for counseling when, after two years of living together, they realized that they did not trust each other enough for a committed relationship. In spite of their mutual distrust, they were in many ways very strongly bound to each other.

The problem for Jane and Harold was that each expected the other to fulfill a fantasy of what a loving partner should do. Consequently, neither could perform perfectly enough to satisfy the other. Jane would ask Harold questions about how he felt, hoping for a particular response. When the desired response was not forthcoming, she was disappointed and he was frustrated. On rare occasions, Harold might respond just the way Jane wanted him to. This only added to Jane's feeling that he was placating her without really meaning what he said!

Aleene helped them by pointing to the dis-ease of their partnership. They had ignored the present "we" by being preoccupied with painful feelings of an unfulfilled past. This limited their ability to trust the unique strengths each had to offer and made each feel incapable of overcoming the other's fears of being disappointed again. Fortunately, Jane and Harold were able to see what Aleene was showing them, making possible an important shift in perspective that resulted in their being able to marry a year later.

Real Partnership Has No Room for Self-sacrifice or Self-absorption

If, as in Jane and Harold's case, we continue to view our partner as someone who must fulfill our deepest longings for connection and friendship, we will perpetuate disappointment and ignore or dismiss those genuine moments of response that are essential to the life of dialogue. It's tragic that in today's western world-view, we exist primarily for ourselves. However this is not a reason for surrendering to the idea that all relationships are selfish and that real partnerships are almost extinct. Pure selfishness is impossible as long as we live our lives in relation to others. Of course I may ask, "What do I get out of it?" I may also ask, "What can I do for you?" Real partnership means we hold "I" and "we" in balance so that neither becomes the sole spokesperson in the life of dialogue.

The parents of Amy Biehl, a 26 year old Fulbright scholar from the United States, exemplify this balance for me. Amy was stoned and stabbed to death in Cape Town, South Africa by black youths, despite the plea of other black youths who were with her in the car that she was a comrade. Amy's parents have forgiven her killers. Her parents spend half their time working in South Africa where they have established an Amy Biehl Foundation for non-violent action. At the Truth and Reconciliation Commission's hearing on amnesty for Amy's killer, Amy's parents met the mother of the 19-year-old who stabbed Amy. She wore an Amy Biehl Foundation T-shirt to her son's amnesty hearing. When the two mothers met, they hugged. Amy herself had often hammered home that you can't blame blacks who had been systematically brutalized under *Apartheid* for turning to violence themselves.

What about the popular altruism in which we deny ourselves and put ourselves aside for the sake of others? Since I bring myself into everything I do, pure altruism is impossible. Even so, when we move to meet each other in a spirit of goodwill and understanding, we find new possibilities for real partnership – often times in situations that seem hostile and intolerable.

Remember the words of the great rabbinic sage, Hillel: "If I am not for myself; who will be for me? If I am for myself alone, what am

25

I? And if not now, when?" This is the "I" that makes real partnership possible. This "I" is revealed poignantly in a number of Hasidic tales. When someone expressed astonishment at Rabbi Moshe Leib of Sasov's capacity to share in another's troubles, he exclaimed: "What do you mean 'share'? It is my own sorrow; how can I help but suffer it?" Equally important for the "I" is being able to speak out for one's own needs. When Rabbi Mendel of Rymanov sat in front of his soup without eating it because the servant had forgotten to give him a spoon, his teacher, Rabbi Elimelekh, remonstrated: "Look, one must know enough to ask for a spoon, and a plate too, if need be!" Mendel, who had always been destitute, heeded this advice, learned to ask, and soon his fortunes mended.

Real Partnership Is Give and Take

How many truly wonderful helpers cannot let themselves be helped? This is how good people end up embittered and "burnt out." They have never realized that receiving is as basic as giving. "As much as the rich man gives the poor man, the poor man gives even more to the rich man," said one Hasidic rabbi.

There is no greater *personal* confirmation that a helper can receive than being allowed by someone to share in the process of healing or teaching him or her. Similarly, there is nothing more disconfirming than wanting to heal or teach someone who resolutely refuses to open herself to real partnership! Even in institutional communities where full mutuality is not possible (like the relationship between doctor and patient) there must still be give and take or no real partnership is possible.

Real Partnership Goes Beyond the Social Contract

The whole notion of social contract that figures so importantly in theories of society from Plato to Hobbes, Rousseau, and John Stuart Mill is based on a split between the individual and society that I believe is a false construct.

Social contract theorists imagine that individuals are bound together socially only by the benefit that accrues to each member of society.

These theorists imply that relationships are mutually exploitive. This is similar to Freud's notion of "mutual" love where each person finds in the other only his or her "cathected love object."

I believe that real partnership involves a different kind of social contact where we become ourselves with one another. A vital reciprocity exists that goes beyond social contracts based on mutual exploitation. When we are living our lives in vital reciprocity so that we become selves *with* one another, we cannot find fulfillment simply by remaining with ourselves or making ourselves the goal. "By never being an end in himself; he endlessly becomes himself." wrote the Chinese philosopher Lao-tzu. Even Abraham Maslow's concept of self-actualization at the center of his psychology of being was only developed *after* he had encountered persons whom he greatly admired, such as Eleanor Roosevelt, Albert Einstein, and Albert Schweitzer, not one of whom was concerned with self-actualization!

Real Partnership Teaches the Wisdom of Responsiveness

To respond wisely we must yield at times and hold our ground at other times. Yielding is often thought to be more virtuous than holding one's ground. Maybe this is because we usually think of one who holds his ground in a relationship as a stubborn individual who is rigid and somewhat defensive. This probably has more to do with how we think about the phrase "holding our ground" than it does with what it actually means to do so. We cannot exist in real partnership with others if we cannot hold our ground. This is because real partnership brings with it the opposition of others to our ideas and ways. When we hold our ground, we maintain our I-ness which includes keeping our unique perspective visible to others. Can you imagine someone like Winston Churchill not holding his ground in the face of resistance to war from his own party members? England might have fallen to the Nazis.

True, we must at times make concessions and yield to the opinions of others. But there is a big difference between yielding judiciously and giving in categorically. There is also a difference between a vulnerable, flexible openness and the kind of self-denial that would force us to surrender our ground so completely that we would be completely overrun by someone else. How do we know when to emphasize yielding and when to emphasize holding our ground? There is no easy formula. The wisdom of responsiveness takes a lifetime of learning. The American poet Theodore Roethke expresses it best with what he calls "the long journey out of the self." Knowing when to hold our ground and when to yield is achieved through real partnership where we go forth again and again to meet others and return again and again to our own centeredness.

Real Partnership Calls for Greater Awareness

A graduate student once approached me about a problem he was having with his girlfriend. He was pressing her to move toward a more serious commitment. Her words agreed, but her actions left him feeling uncertain about how serious she really was. It was clear to me from what he told me that she was not serious about him. It was also clear to me that he could not see that she was relating to him on several levels.

Relationships are seldom simple and almost always very complex. We sometimes try to simplify what we view as complexity in another person by focusing on one dimension of their personality. This is because it makes us feel anxious to think that a potential partner is not all of one mind. What if the student's girlfriend had said, "I am not ready to make a greater emotional commitment to 'us' but I don't want to lose the level of intimacy that we have?" That might have left him feeling too ambiguous to maintain a status quo until her feelings deepened.

In my personal and professional experience, the awareness we can't bear to hold in focus usually comes into the circle of our consciousness through dreams, fantasies, memories, twinges of pain or embarrassment. These are oblique visitations. They are valuable and important because they often help us develop a tolerance for greater (and sometimes more painful) awareness. The greater our awareness of the multi-dimensional ways we relate to people and they to us, the more we can respond to the whole of what appears through the life of dialogue.

There is a direct relationship between my being more fully aware and how I respond to you. This is true even when you do not express yourself to me in words. When I am fully aware, I can ask myself if there is something you are trying to tell me. Even when I find your silence uncomfortable, I can make an effort to be helpful and genuine in my response to you.

This applies even to those difficult relationships where we might find ourselves falsely accused and unfairly treated. Unfair treatment could be a genuine, albeit distorted, cry for help. People are often mistaken when they think that objectivity makes it possible to respond with compassion and understanding, to someone who is striking out viciously due to deep inner pain. Objectivity (clinical or otherwise) by definition is too impersonal to allow the kind of responsiveness I am talking about. Rabbi Shelomo of Karlin found the narrow ridge between the two in a Hasidic tale called "Climbing Down":

Rabbi Shelomo said: "If you want to raise a man from the mud and filth, do not think it is enough to keep standing on top and reaching down to him a helping hand. You must go all the way down yourself, down into the mud and filth. Then take hold of him with strong hands and pull him and yourself out into the light."[1]

Real Partnership Is Listening and Responding

Listening and responding at a greater depth is a bold step away from specious individualism towards real partnership. The person who listens and does not respond is more observer than participant. When we fail to respond in the interest of self-protection, we thicken the distance between our unique existences, creating a false sense of security by telling ourselves we are not like those poor suffering folks over there.

The life of dialogue is diminished when we fail to see that we are all in the same boat, headed toward the same waterfall, sharing the same fate. Franz Rosenzweig pointed out that true dialogue means that we have not only ears but also a mouth. I can say something surprising, new, unique, and unrepeatable that evokes a spontaneous and unprepared response from you. When this happens, both hearer and speaker are called to new depths of awareness. Real partnership depends on real listening and real responding. How many times have you found that you could not be moved by someone who speaks to you as though from a script? Isn't this the reason we hang up on telemarketers and turn the channel away from televangelists? When real listening as well as real talking takes place, we can't help but be stirred to think and prodded to act. Stirring and prodding, when a byproduct of real listening and responding, lead to the real partnerships that empower family, community, and society.

Real Partnership Leads to Personal Transformation

People whose trust is grounded in the life of dialogue are changed every time they enter into real partnership. They are reborn in each new situation. By listening and responding with greater awareness, we help in this process of rebirth. Personal transformation occurs as a result of being a participant in real partnership; it is not a goal we must achieve in order to become full participants. The difference is hardly subtle. We change because we respond wholeheartedly when someone comes to meet us. We may still need to exercise our will in order to overcome certain obstacles. We will also have to allow ourselves to be taken up into the flowing interaction without knowing the outcome.

To our own surprise, we discover resources we did not know we had or give voice to deep convictions that we timidly hid. We may even become aware that what we are doing is not what we are called to do. One man told me that after years in two professions, each requiring a great deal of education and training, he walked away from both convinced that neither profession was in sync with what he knew to be his true life's direction.

One additional and important distinction needs to be made with respect to personal wholeness. Any time I view myself self-consciously I lose my intuitive grasp of the person that I am. This means I cannot achieve personal wholeness by being self-conscious. Endless self-preoccupation splits us into two parts (like Dostoevsky's "Underground Man," "twiddling his thumbs" and totally unable to act), one of which is the observer and the other the actor who is being observed. This kind of self-splitting prevents us from having any sort of spontaneous response and burdens us unnecessarily with self-consciousness.

Does this mean we must abandon objectivity, analysis and self-awareness? To do so would be a self-conscious effort to do the right thing in order to be a more whole person – exactly the opposite of what I am suggesting. The intuitive awareness that comes in responding is not incompatible with objectivity, analysis, or even psychoanalysis. But it *is* incompatible with making these forms of self-evaluation the final court of appeal as to what makes partnerships real.

We need an awareness of ourselves when relating to others. Self-awareness ensures that we maintain a balance between complete detachment and unhealthy immersion. We grow more intuitive with respect to the subtle changes in the life of dialogue as we both listen and respond; hearing not just how the other responds but also how we ourselves respond to him. When I discuss a problem with a friend, I not only hear her but I also hear myself responding to her. Intuitively, I am watching the back and forth between us and, like learning the steps to a ballroom dance, becoming more adept at timing my listening and responding self with hers.

T. S. Eliot captures this experience beautifully, "When the music is heard so deeply that you are the music while the music lasts." Naturally, our self-consciousness returns when the music stops, but it need not get in the way as much as we often think. The Hasidic Maggid of Mezritch said to his disciples that they must say Torah in such a way that the Universe of the Word speaks through them. But "as soon as you hear yourself speaking, you must stop."

Every gifted performer knows that we must have only a light self-consciousness instead of a heavy one. To learn how to handle our self-consciousness lightly, we must avoid the mistake of imagining that our real self is only the knower. The more we do that, the more we prevent ourselves from entering into real partnerships. The followers of one Hasidic *rebbe* could not understand what riveted his gaze to the foolish spectacle of a rope dancer. "This man is risking his life, and I don't know why," he replied when questioned. "But I am sure he is not thinking of the hundred gulden he will get at the end of the performance, for if he did he would fall."

CHAPTER 3

Obstacles, Barriers, Challenges to Real Partnership

The Bakancing Act of Standing Our Ground

We lack the wholeness that makes real partnership possible when we do not have the courage to stand our ground and make our unique personal witness in response to the situation before us. And yet, we risk losing the esteem of others when we do. During the time of the Viet Nam War I was invited to lecture at a small college by a young English professor who had read my books *Problematic Rebel* and *To Deny Our Nothingness*. I was astonished by the enthusiasm he evinced in his letters before he had even met me, particularly when in his third letter he declared that they (he and a small group of younger professors) loved me. Like me, the English professors and his young colleagues opposed the Viet Nam War. When I arrived at the campus I was taken to see the secret underground newspaper run by these more radical young professors.

Later, a luncheon was held for me where I met the senior professor in the Department of English. He expressed himself as for the Vietnam War. I questioned his facts and in general took him to task. It was my intention to be direct without being either abrasive or rude. That night after my lecture to the whole college the young professor who had invited me did not come to the party held for me. This disturbed me so much that I called him up and urged him to come, which he did. I discovered that he was upset because I had challenged the professor who had authority over him. Even though he agreed with my position on the war, he had not widened his stance sufficiently to stand his ground when the unexpected happened. His fear of losing his job and status left him with no faith in developing real partnership with me, whom he admired, or with his senior colleague for whom he had respect but could not imagine meeting in genuine dialogue.

To meet others and to hold our ground when we meet them is one of the most difficult tasks in the world. And yet our becoming whole cannot happen unless we summons the courage to do just that. Not merely one time or a few times, but again and again in each lived moment. If you are preoccupied with your self-esteem or with your image of how you appear to others, you will not stand your ground for fear of losing their approval. This was clearly at the root of the younger English professor's sudden withdrawal.

Because we are invested in the way others see us, we tend to alternate between two opposite forms of *almost* meeting: "meeting" others through leaving our ground *or* "protecting" our own ground through closing ourselves off and holding others at arm's length. In the first case, we take on other people's thoughts and feelings while losing our own. In order to avoid being shut out, we put our own attitudes on a back burner. In the second case, we act as though we are certain we will be rejected and give such forceful expression to our own touchstones of reality that we make no room for another point of view. Our unhappiness is often rooted in our inability to meet others while holding our ground. We have either remained too hidden or too defensive to discover the unique opportunities presented in daily living.

It is in the wisdom of our own daily living that we discover the right swinging movement between meeting others and standing our ground. As much as we want to make openness or loving others a principle, we can't without severely limiting our ability to be genuinely outgoing and spontaneous. In fact, being committed to principles for principle's sake can lead us to taking stands where our own opinions and resistance to being persuaded can make it nearly impossible for genuine dialogue to unfold. Whether we impose upon ourselves an idea of what we ought to do or avoid spontaneous interaction with others in hope of maintaining an image of self-sufficiency, we face the same unhappy outcome.

"Yes, I agree." you say. "But I hate conflict. Surely there is a way to avoid conflict and still meet others in a genuine dialogue." The wish to avoid conflict is one major reason people do not have the courage to stand their ground. If you fear your friend, lover or teacher may become a critical or rejecting person the moment you reveal your true attitudes, you will propitiate and conciliate in an effort to maintain a "comfortable" relationship. But the truth is the exact opposite. By giving up your ground in an effort to be conciliatory and maintain a status quo, you come into direct conflict with that person. It may not be apparent at first, but over time the "comfortable" relationship you have sacrificed your ground to create feels stagnant, distant and unrewarding. Your failure to respond as a whole person by standing your ground only postpones an inevitable conflict.

There is a way you can truly *avoid* coming into relational conflict. Stand your ground in such a way as to remain open to your friend's point of view. When you imagine her side of the relationship while letting her see your side, you avoid letting your friend think that you are going along with her freely and gladly while, underneath, the resentment builds up.

Albert Camus' great novel *The Stranger* is an excellent example of this. Walking on the beach, the heat becomes for Meursault an unbearable pressure that leads him to shoot an Arab as a desperate revolt–-a breaking of an unendurable tension. What has happened here is nothing other than Meursault's mourning for his mother. That he did not weep at her funeral was not because of hard-heartedness but because he identifies himself with her. Like her, he expects nothing of the world. This lack of expectation is the clue to his seeming indifference to life. It is not that he wants nothing, but that–-aside from a few immediate physical sensations–-he hopes for nothing. He is a man who has schooled himself never to demand anything of life, never to expect anything of it. Like the rebel whom Camus describes in the book of that title, Meursault "confronts an order of things which oppresses him with the insistence on a kind of right not to be oppressed beyond the limit that he can tolerate." This is not a conscious decision on Meursault's part but the limit that the self sets to the vast, indifferent nothingness that crushes it out of existence.[2]

Most of us will never shoot someone, but we all let out more anger or irritation than the occasion demands because we have consistently failed to stand our ground on other occasions.

There Are Real Impasses That Prevent Real Partnership

Our response to a particular situation often gets us in touch with real limits that may prevent the deepening of a partnership we imagine we want. Much to our frustration, we experience tragedies of miscommunication and mismeeting along with moments of insurmountable opposition on the part of others. One woman said, "I really hoped counseling would help my husband and me resolve our conflict and help us to be more loving. I see now how far apart we really are. Even if we could begin to understand one another, I fear neither of us has the resources to bridge the gap that exists between us."

I was touched by a story in which a Bosnian soldier, after capturing a Serbian soldier, recognized him as a childhood classmate and friend from the village from which all the Bosnians had fled except for his father. "I am sorry to tell you that your father is not alive," the Serbian told the Bosnian. The latter knew this meant that the Serbians had shot him. The Serbian soldier reminded the Bosnian of their childhood friendship and asked, "Do you think there is any hope for the Serbs and the Bosnians?" "Yes," replied his captor, "but not for you and me" and shot him.

In light of the fact that such impasses exist in the world, should we abandon the search for real partnership? It is not possible to express conflict and hostility in every relationship. It depends very much upon the amount and kind of hostility that is expressed and the strength of the relationship. There are some relationships that have so little resources that as soon as the volcano of hostility threatens to erupt, the relationship comes undone with no possibility of recovery.

Other relationships are too fragile to tolerate even the slightest discomfort. I can recall one family who came to me because they were having problems with their thirteen-year-old son. He was having difficulty bonding with his stepmother though she had been his primary care giver since he was five. She grew increasingly demanding that he respond to her care giving. She was so fixed in her own benevolent image that they she was terrified to show any other face. Consequently, her care giving became smothering to the young man. When he elected to go live with his real mother, she rejected him completely.

We discover perilous impasses in the very relationships we hope will work and there are no formulae that can help us in tragic situations. While I worked feverishly to find a solution for this young man and his family, he repeatedly insisted I was wasting my time. He knew something that I did not want to accept--that I often have to choose in a particular situation between my affinity to one person and responsibility to another. Because I am often in relationship with more than one person at any one time, I frequently find myself caught in genuine dilemmas between affinity and responsibility that are not easy to resolve. I can even feel torn between my love for one person and my loyalty to another who may be at odds with the former. I can give only so much. While I would not deliberately shut someone out, I cannot be there for everybody. This leads to the realization that, in spite of my efforts to be inclusive, someone in relationship to me will feel shut out.

Part of our coming to terms with impasses in relationships is the realization that we can never *wholly* take responsibility for anyone because we do not have the resources to do so. Even when we are the only person on earth to whom our friend can turn, our resources to respond run out before the need is satisfied. We can only really help others if we recognize the limits of the grace of each hour. Honest relationship leads to a growing sureness about what we can give and what we cannot. When we go out to meet one another as limited people, likely to make mistakes and certain to meet with disappointments, we can enter into real partnership.

Things and People Are Not Always As They Seem

This leads to a second complexity when discussing real partnerships. Things and people are not always as they seem. The impression you have of me as an author may differ greatly from the impression you have after meeting me in person. I have already pointed out that an essential problem in relationships is the desperate need for confirmation that leads us to try to appear a certain way to win the approval of others. How do we deal with the fact that we want to influence others favorably and not fall into the trap of being so preoccupied with how we appear to others that we mask our thoughts, opinions and ideas? The masked person is the "seeming" person who lets seeming creep between himself and others so that no real sharing of thoughts, ideas, and attitudes takes place. In real partnerships, "truth" does not mean saying whatever comes to mind and exposing oneself before another but granting that person a share in one's being.

It is not inherently difficult to be genuine, but we may have many strong justifications for why we shouldn't be our true selves to the world. Real partnership demands that we face our concerns and allow our response to the situation to reveal our true self with those who address us. I had a long-time friend from the days of Civilian Public Service who, at my suggestion to the College, had joined me as a colleague at Sarah Lawrence College. He was a dedicated pacifist and a serious philosopher. Nonetheless, there was an unmistakable element of seeming in him. One time he was talking to me and I distinctly saw two aspects — the one that wished to appear sincere in the direct frontal view and the mocking one on the side. This certainly affected my impression of him as a person. I believe that people are polar and that the polarity is not good at one end and evil at the other. Instead, on one end there lie moments of decision where we choose a direction because we must be true to ourselves. On the other end lies an aimless whirl where we refuse to commit ourselves or commit half-heartedly for fear of taking a position we know will result in our being labeled, judged, or exposed.

The Problem With Mistrust and Real Partnership

The Holocaust that led to the extermination of six million unique persons exceeds our capacity to understand or even imagine. We are still dealing with its aftermath more than fifty years later. To name only one, we live in a time when the most ordinary social confidence is no longer present. We could not imagine, in advance, that people would systematically turn other persons into cakes of soap or irradiate people in such a way that they would die on the spot *or* slowly and horribly over a great many years, or that two of the world's tallest buildings could be razed, killing over three thousand, by two airplanes in broad daylight while we watched in stunned disbelief. When the unbelievable happens, reality creates possibility, and the outrageous is no longer unthinkable.

The era of Auschwitz, Hiroshima, Viet Nam, the Gulag Archipelago is our reality; we have witnessed the horrors in Cambodia, Ethiopia, South Africa and, more recently, the Gulf War, Somalia, Bosnia, Afghanistan, and the genocide in Darfur plus the second war in Iraq, which our government falsely tried to sell us on the grounds that Iraq had weapons of mass destruction and that Saddam Hussein was in league with Osama bin Laden the architect of 9/11, both of which claims President Bush and Vive=President Cheyney later admitted were not true. The thawing of the Cold War and the tumbling of the Berlin wall notwithstanding, nuclear weapons are accessible to tiny countries and well-funded terrorists. I have spoken in some of my other works of a "Dialogue with the Absurd" in which we can find meaning even in absurd encounters. But that does not mean that the inconceivable horror that it has been our fate to witness and live through is anything other than just that. There can be no meaningful philosophy that enables us to be comfortable with the destruction and endless suffering of countless of our contemporaries.

We have to do with all of what is pointed out above and with the loss of trust in our meetings with others in personal, social, and political realms. So much of our energy goes into proving to one another that our motives and intentions are good. Still we doubt others and grow weary of their doubts toward us. My friend Abraham Joshua Heschel coined a "Golden Rule" to match the mistrust of our times: "Suspect thy neighbor as thyself!" We no longer really believe that we can enter into real partnership. There are periods in history such as the present when the meeting with present reality in the everyday is lost in a welter of personal and social distrust. The fact that we have a ground to stand on means nothing if much of what we experience is not at all as it seems, even after we have made every effort to be genuine.

"Basic trust" lies in the integral relationship between the life of dialogue and real partnerships that make true community a reality. The life of dialogue and real partnership can only be expressed when we have the "the courage to address and the courage to respond." Trustworthiness in real partnership means recognizing that other people do not possess fixed character — good or evil, honest or dishonest — but that the way in which we approach them, the way in which we allow life to flow between us and them, frees them to possibilities of goodness, trust, and openness. Distrust or the lack of basic trust puts people in categories that make it difficult for them to break out of habitual modes of dishonesty and self-protection. When I approach you with openness and trust, you may be able to respond in kind. When I approach you with hatred and distrust, you will be confirmed as having no real role in a relationship where we could otherwise work together to solve problems, build understanding, and find a common ground from which to relate.

The terrible thing about mistrust is that it quickly becomes reciprocal. If we reflect suspicion on someone else, it is reflected back on us until we find the very evidence we are looking for: the other also mistrusts us and acts in ways to confirm our worst fears about him. The hyper-suspicious behavior of large groups and societies in relation to one another is exactly what we would call paranoid if we encountered it in individuals. We don't have to go very far to see how this is true after September 11th, 2001, when we are being encouraged by our government and its leaders to be watchful for the terrorist in our midst.

Many groups (even mainstream ones) have a shut-in, closed world, sealed off from seeing in the way that the other sees. Each tends to interpret the motives of the other in terms of its own world of defenses, fears, and suspicions. This is patently true not only of many of today's religious sects the world over, whether "born-again Christians," orthodox Hasidim, or fundamentalist Muslims, but also of secular organizations and governments. The secular fundamentalism that seems to dominate American politics is not so different from the religious sects in Israel that demand that all civil functions, such as weddings and funerals, be dictated by the Orthodox at the expense of the non-orthodox (secularist, Reform, and Conservative Jew alike).

The Need For Greater Trust in Response to Mistrust

Only trust gives us the footing we need to stand in the face of mistrust. In other words, you ought not respond to mistrust with mistrust. Nor can we establish a prescribed response to mistrust in an effort to protect our self-interest. Our responses are those that we find in the moment where we encounter mistrust. It is very much like a person who starts walking in a direction, gets knocked down so the breath is knocked out of her, and then has to choose whether to get up and keep walking in the same direction or to stop altogether. Trust does not lead to "peace of mind" or "peace of soul." The act of trusting can result in pain, grief and anxiety. When I stop trusting, I put an end to the life of dialogue. "The broken heart it kens nae second spring again, thae the waeful nae cease frae their greeting," says the third stanza of the familiar song "Loch Lomond."

There are some people who continue to live, yet never really trusting anyone or thing. A good example of this is the movie *The Pawnbroker* where Rod Steiger plays a Jewish pawnbroker in Harlem who lost his wife and son in a Nazi extermination camp and from then on had established his business but shut his heart away from life so as not to risk further disappointment and loss. Is there not, says the poet Conrad Aiken, one "tetelestai" (forsaken) that can be said for those "who creep through life guarding their hearts from blows to die obscurely?" Who would presume to judge them? Are not they, in their so different way, like Jesus who cried out his "forsaken!" on the cross?

But our desire for security leads some of us to see ourselves as forsaken simply because life does not comport itself as we think it should. We wish to prescribe what will come to us and, like Kafka's mole, construct a burrow that will make it sure that nothing reaches us except what we want to reach us. Our views of existence are based upon our disappointments, upon the shattering of trust that every child experiences no matter how confirming his or her parents are. Every child experiences separation and betrayal to some degree. And later, when growing up and first entering into romantic relations, every person experiences some rejection and hurt. Time and time again we think that we have "had it," yet at another moment we are able, like a character in Samuel Beckett's novels, to get up and go on.

Without a doubt relationships wound, maim and sometimes kill. They also confirm, heal and often times bring great comfort and joy. I have said to those who believe they are most secure when least affected by others that wounds sustained in relationships must be healed in relationships. Prolonged, self-imposed isolation for the sake of staying safe turns a small wound into a huge barrier so that even when you want to try to reach out to someone and risk again you will find yourself unable to break through your fear. More than we can conceive, we are sustained from the life of dialogue and real partnership itself. To be sure, the experience is not smooth and continuous. Yet our participation and decisions to trust again renew and empower us. We walk near the abyss at every moment; we walk in the valley of the shadow of death every day. Yet moment-by-moment we are carried; day-by-day we are given back our ground and our freedom. Distrust, no matter how deep, need not prevent our making new contact with reality. If we dare to trust, we will find that true community is the only place to find real partnership.

PART TWO

SUSTAINING REAL PARTNERSHIP THROUGH ACTIVE CARING

CHAPTER 4

The Caring Community and the Commune Movement

The Youth Rebellion of the 60's and 70's

The 1960s and 1970s were years of social activism—some would say social revolution. Along with the great strides made toward racial equality, women's liberation, protests against the Vietnam War, and the "greening of America" in general there was also a rebellion against authority that made itself felt on a great many college campuses and public arenas in America. The spirit of community that I found at Pendle Hill was not quite sufficient to sustain it during that rebellion. At Pendle Hill too the rebellion against authority was often carried to absurdity by young people wanting to prove themselves at the expense of the institution. Once when we organized a Pendle Hill Seminar, our attempts to have meetings of the whole community addressed by a great university professor were disrupted by students pounding the benches and shouting at him, a fellow Pendle Hiller like themselves. "Who do you think you are? God?" This was not a protest against him in particular or even against the institution. It was a rejection of anyone who presumed to speak with authority.

Our smaller gatherings met with no better fate. In one group that I led, two Pendle Hillers attempted to conduct a session on some of the problems they had encountered as psychiatric social workers. Soon, however, the session was taken over by three young men who were part of the group. One was a Nietzschean romantic, one was a self-styled Zen Buddhist, and one was a self-styled Tibetan Buddhist. When, after an hour of silence on my part, I finally decided to intervene on behalf of the group, the Nietzchean clapped his hands above his head repeatedly and claimed that I was interrupting him. The Tibetan Buddhist kindly explained to me later that I was "irrelevant." In those days that meant the young people set the agenda and the elders had nothing meaningful to say.

In a last ditch effort to save the Pendle Hill Seminar I was directing, I organized students into smaller groups of three to see if they could have any real meeting with one another. To my despair, the results were no better. One of the two mature women whom I had chosen to meet with began our session by saying to me, "I want to get this off my chest. You're irrelevant," to which the other added, "You're not a person. You're a bag of quotations!" This made me wonder whether any real meeting at all was possible.

In spite of student protests and the rebellion of those years, there were some real gains in the realization of a caring community at Pendle Hill, such as interest groups started and conducted by various students and participation of the faculty and students in decision making. Many of these gains have been "corrected" in subsequent years in the name of making Pendle Hill a more truly "Quaker" institution. Even at the height of Pendle Hill as a caring and confirming community, there was always a certain measure of fear and mistrust of uncomfortable voices--a mistrust that expressed itself by the board going into "executive" session at regular intervals, at which point they excluded the faculty members of the board. In all genuine communities, there is a tension between convention and innovation. But the limits that are set often grow out of fear rather than genuine necessity.

The Commune Movement

A high point of Pendle Hill as a caring community was the *National Conference on Communes and Underground Churches* that

Barbara Krasner and I organized and co-directed in the summer of 1969. At that moment we were able to touch the pulse of a great striving for caring community that manifested itself in many different places and forms during those years. At the same time there were aspects of this conference that showed the limits to the comm.unity's resources for confirming otherness. There were minor problems with people who wanted to park their campers on Pendle Hill grounds and the surprising defection of one of the members of the planning committee to an alternative conference that suddenly arose out of nowhere. A more serious issue arose when the wife of a local black leader pointed out that, although communes had a lot to offer the black population of Philadelphia and other great cities, the blacks in general did not have the leisure that would make the imagining and planning of such communes possible. I felt that what she said was true and I could not offer any helpful alternative.

In spite of this, a hundred people gathered from around the country who really cared about these issues. So far as I know, this conference was unique. I took away a sense of what the commune movement was about.

There are still many communes in America, and in that sense there is still a commune movement. Some of these communes were centered on drugs, some on radical politics, some on religion, some on sexual freedom or nudity; some were city communes and some were agricultural. Despite the eccentric nature of some communes, there were and are communes that manifest genuine community. All of them represented interesting experiments in intentional community; a few of them demonstrated an ability to last beyond the cultural milieu that created them and endure in the later, more conservative era that followed.

During the *1950s* I came to know the historian Staughton Lynd. Staughton carried the political liberalism of his parents, Helen and Robert Lynd, into the social sphere by joining Macedonia, an intentional community in Georgia. Macedonia, like the Celo Community in North Carolina (founded by Arthur Morgan of the TVA), was one of the few successful agricultural communes in the

South that lasted over several decades. It was an organic community, but it was also a democracy.

It was with some dismay, therefore, that I learned that Macedonia had been taken over by the *Bruderhof*. The *Bruderhof* was a religious community, or rather group of related communities, originally founded by Eberhard Arnold in Germany after the First World War. The *Bruderhof* is an excellent illustration of what Martin Buber said in *Paths in Utopia* about the need for federation of communes, but its methods leave something to be desired as far as genuine community is concerned. It is, in fact, a cult--a not too well concealed theocracy in which the decisions are made by a small group of leaders at the center. This applies not only to the taking over of Macedonia and the running of their communities at Reston, New York, and elsewhere, but also to the private lives of their members. The leaders decided that Stoughton had to separate from his wife and saw that that was done.

CHAPTER 5

Genuine Community:
The Community of Affinity versus
the Community of Otherness

Pendle Hill—The Quaker Study Center

My most important experience in community during the *50s,* 60s, and early 70s was my years of living and teaching at Pendle Hill, the Quaker study center in Wallingford, Pennsylvania, about which I spoke in the previous chapter. There was structure and order at Pendle Hill, yet there was individual freedom in the deepest sense. There were attempts to build real community between the staff and the one-year residents through common work, common study, common prayer — the daily silent meeting for worship in the barn, and the Friends Business Meetings that were carried out according to the "sense of the meeting" rather than majority vote and parliamentary rules. The spirit of community also carried over to the volley ball court where poor players and children were accorded equal rights with good players and adults.

The Spirit of Sameness vs. the Spirit of Otherness

To understand the authentication of the human in community and society, my distinction between the "community of affinity"

49

and genuine community—the community that confirms otherness--needs to be elaborated.

The community of *affinity,* or *like-mindedness,* is based on what people feel they have in common — race, sex, religion, nationality, politics, a common formula, a common creed. Genuine community, in contrast, does not mean that everyone does the same thing and certainly not that they do it from the same point of view. What makes community real is people finding themselves in a common situation — a situation that they approach in different ways yet which calls each of them out. The very existence in genuine community is already a common concern, a caring for one another. This caring begins with understanding from within the actual people present. Only then does it extend to gather other people in and then to a dialogue with other communities.

Any group activity is an example of this since it naturally splits up into people who do one task and people who do another. But beyond that, if people care about community, they can build it together even if they have different creeds, philosophies, or world-views.

To some extent I think that was true of the faculty at Sarah Lawrence College during the fourteen years I taught there. They were certainly enormously varied in attitude, viewpoint, philosophy, and creed, if any. Yet they all cared about the Sarah Lawrence way of teaching and worked together to make it succeed. This was true of the students as well.

When natural disasters occur, people who would not otherwise be counted as "like-minded" pull together for the benefit of the community. When we look carefully, we see that variegated communities are everywhere: the Green Party, the Rainbow Coalition, the United Nations to name a few.

Genuine Community

Most communities come into being through the grouping together of people who have something in common. Yet the community of affinity will ultimately become exclusive and closed unless it evolves into genuine community, faithful and diverse at the same time. The ultimate context of real partnership is genuine community where there exists lived togetherness of truly unique persons, families and groups Genuine communities comes into being not simply through tolerance, adjustment, and compromise but through mutual confirmation.

It is beyond human capacity to confirm all otherness. But the genuine community should be measured by the otherness that it can confirm. If the "spokesman" of the group explains to someone who differs with him or her that that person is really not a member of the group because he or she does not fit the general stamp of the group, then that person will not only have been read out of the group, but out of existence itself as far as this moment and this situation are concerned. The obverse attitude is that of openness and trust. It is our lack of basic trust that makes us feel that we need to have the security of groups based on generalized affinity, rather than the concreteness of open meeting with real otherness that is present in every group, down to a pair of friends or a husband and wife.

A remarkable example of meaningful interconnectedness is *Gnadenthal* — a small German community an hour's drive from Frankfurt. *Gnadenthal* (Valley of Grace) is the home of the *Jesus-Brudersehaft* for which I once served as the sole faculty for a summer institute with students from ten different countries. Each successive visit since that time has deeply impressed us with the spirit of community that exists there.

We came to *Gnadenthal* at the invitation of Jens Oertel — my student at the Hebrew University of Jerusalem when I was senior Fulbright lecturer there in 1987-1988. Jens' s father Gunter Oertel is the director of the *Jesus-Brudersehaft* that now has communities in three different parts of Germany as well as in Israel and Africa. In his essay "Places of Hope," Jen' s father Gunter Oertel gave beautiful expression to this communal spirit. "Places of hope can arise," he said, "where new interhuman relationships grow and the external reality of life is given shape." He then pointed to the genuine meeting of persons of different origins, coinage, and language. Aware of the secular world that surrounds each of their communities, he nonetheless expressed confidence that their way of life can build bridges to persons who are oriented to a completely different world of values. "The essence of life — that we have learned from Martin Buber —is meeting, dialogue."

In community, this means wanting to meet and understand the other as the person facing us, as Thou. Thus community unfolds in a basic rhythm of hearing and speaking, receiving and giving. Despite the economic crisis and the massive unemployment in East Germany, a dozen persons who had been without work for a long time were established in a firm work-relationship in *Hennersdorf,* the Jesus *Bruderschaft* community in East Germany.

Another remarkable example of community that I came on is a Minnesota system of justice that substitutes a community circle for the traditional court that sentences criminals. Reasoning that jails and judges do not prevent people from committing crimes again and again, circle advocates suggest giving trust and kind impulses of ordinary citizens a try. They feel that by deferring always to professionals, we have robbed the judicial process of the wisdom and insight of the community. Community circles draw on that wisdom to craft unconventional sentences meant to be more instructive than punitive. Melissa, a 14-year-old who ran away repeatedly from her rural Minnesota home, was sentenced to write down five good things about each day. Melissa's parents commented that in court they had encountered only harried lawyers and intimidating judges whereas in circle "they found a dozen neighbors they'd never met before who are pulling for Melissa to reform—-and, most important, who genuinely believe she can do it."

Although the circles also include judges and lawyers and professionals of other kinds, in the circles they are only a part of the group and speak with no special authority. One member characterized the circles as giving the little people, the common folk, some responsibility for making sure that their community is safe and that their neighbors are held accountable. Tracing the idea of circles back to Native American tradition, advocates point out that crimes are not simply violations of abstract laws. They are also affronts to the community. "So it should be up to the community to hold the offender responsible ---and to figure out a way to bring him back into the fold."

The only rule that holds for circles is that they do not act like juries. They deal only with offenders who have pleaded guilty. Beyond that the key to the circle is first-name equality and consensus. Everyone, including the applicant or offender, must agree with every condition of the sentence, which is usually community service. The victim too joins in the discussion, but only as a community member not an accusing witness.

Although judges review the sentences, the circles represent a deliberate rejection of the adversarial system. "It's not shame, blame and off you go." Citizens willing to counsel a crook week after week have a passion for rehabilitation that sets them in greatest contrast with the members of society who are bent on three-strike laws and ever-tougher prisons. The rate of recidivism is remarkably low. One statistic shows offenders who completed circles as committing 82% fewer crimes. Acknowledging that circles are not appropriate for criminals who present a real danger to the community, circle advocates think they can handle aggressors, including some sexual offenders.

Circle members work hard to mentor offenders——writing their resumes or putting them up in a spare bedroom. Circles have even spread to the schools where school counselors now convene student circles to deal with playground disputes. Some communities hold "healing circles" where crime victims can talk through their trauma with neighbors or even confront the perpetrators who harmed them.[3]

CHAPTER 6

The Role Personal Direction Plays in Real Partnership

Finding personal direction does not mean, as people think finding a way to express our inner creativity or genius or even to work out one's personal destiny, as if it were a predestined something inside of us that only needs to be brought out into the open. Rather it entails many years of meaningful interaction with the persons with whom we have to do in our families, our schools, and our places of work. It is also co-constituted by the places in which we live, the natural world that we come up against in our ordinary lives and in our "escapes" from these lives in what we call our "vacations." It means, in short, not expression of our inwardness but meaningful dialogue with what is not ourselves to which we bring ourselves again and again with all the resources that we can muster in each given situation and with such personal wholeness as we can bring to bear on that situation.

Finding Personal Direction in Learning and Teaching

We do not learn in the first instance from reading books but from our life in our families, our meetings with our teachers, and even from our interactions with our classmates. But this first learning is so primordial and so much a part of the shaping of our original characters that we are not consciously aware of it, much less seeing it as part of finding personal direction. After we have learned how to read and later to think for ourselves, we can catch glimpses of how our learning is affecting our personal directions.

I had one such glimpse from the course in American history that I took in high school. A few years later when I decided to become a conscientious objector to the Second World War while an undergraduate at Harvard College, I wrote my high school American history teacher asking her whether she would vouch for my sincerity to my draft board. She declined to do so – not, I am sure, because she doubted my sincerity since I was her prize pupil and also one she saw as having a "lovely social consciousness." When I went to see her after my sophomore year at Harvard and told her that I had made all A's, she declared that this was a "national honor." Perhaps she was shocked that her teaching should have led, or contributed, to such a stand on my part or possibly she feared that to witness for me would endanger her own position as a teacher at Tulsa Central High School. But I am quite sure that I would not have asked her, alone out of all my high school teachers, to witness for me if I had not thought that the American history she taught me and her way of teaching it had made a meaningful contribution to my decision to become a C. O.

I did not mention this course when I wrote a long letter explaining my stand to my draft board. What I did speak of was the effect on me of reading the novels of Dostoyevsky and of that scene in Tolstoy's *War and Peace* in which Prince Andre, lying wounded on the battlefield, He looks up at the sky and has a glimpse of eternity that lifts him out of the war that has engrossed him totally until then. This was a book that I had read as a sophomore in the comparative novel class taught by Harry Levin at Harvard though, given the far more impersonal relationship of professors to students at Harvard, I would never have dreamed of asking him to write in my behalf, grateful though I was to him for having directed me to read both Dostoyevsky and Tolstoy. I think, in contrast, that I was influenced more directly by what Esther Larson brought to teaching American history than by the textbook itself, even though I prided myself on being able to open any page of that several-hundred-page textbook and know what was in it. Both teachers contributed to my, often anguished, decision to become a conscientious objector--an important step, certainly in my finding my personal life direction.

I have adduced two specific learnings that influenced my personal life direction. I should also mention studying in the Progressive Education Thirty School Experiment in junior and senior high schools and the fine liberal arts education at Harvard both of which provided me with open approaches to ideas and to history and a habit of penetrating thought. Worthy of mention too is my taking part in an international student service work camp between my sophomore and junior years at Harvard, for it was this experience that brought me to change my personal direction from training to be in international diplomacy to hopefully become active in the labor movement. With this in mind I changed my major to Economics my junior year at Harvard and graduated with a *magna cum laude* in labor economics. I was not able to continue in this direction after my three-and-a-half years in Civilian Public Service camps; for during which time I went from socialism and a somewhat intellectual pacifism to mysticism and later still to a great sympathy with the popular communal Jewish mysticism of eighteenth-and-nineteenth century Eastern Europe known as Hasidism.

When l went on weekends to Philadelphia during my year and a half in an "institute for the feeble minded," as such places were then called, I got to know a very fine European intellectual, both older and better educated than I was, who assured me that after the war I would return to the labor economics and social reform that I had chosen as my personal direction while in college. He was mistaken. I could not go back to economics or to my plans to become a labor organizer or educator. Instead I earned an M.A. in English from Ohio State University. (This change of major was noted against me on my transcript by the committee in Oklahoma City after Harvard College nominated me for a Rhodes scholarship.) Rather than stay with English, moreover, I got a Ph.D. in the History of Culture from the University of Chicago, ending my academic career as professor in three separate departments: Religious Studies, Philosophy, and

Comparative Literature. This does not mean, however, that my work in economics or my social concern were simply tossed overboard. I have remained a communal socialist throughout my life, and this has affected my approach to all the social and political problems that have confronted me during that half-century.

My varied academic background and the varied approaches to education that accompanied it have had, of course, a great effect on my approach to teaching during the more than half century that I have taught in colleges and universities large and small, liberal, progressive, and conservative. A dean at Sarah Lawrence College—a small progressive women's college where I taught for fourteen years— said to me that I would have to choose between straight courses and the "mixed bags" that I tended to teach. I chose the latter. At Temple University in Philadelphia I founded and directed Ph.D. programs in Religion and Literature and in Religion and Psychology. At the California School for Professional Psychology in San Diego where I was on the core faculty for two years I instituted a whole new track of "non-statistical"—phenomenological, theoretical, and case study— doctoral dissertations that no one at that institution had dreamed of before. I have also taught in a number of universities without walls that have left room for individual tutoring and phenomenological dissertations.

Throughout those years I have steadily grown in my conviction that meaningful education is one of dialogue between teachers and students, students with one another, and students with the books that they read. This has meant for me preferring small classes to large, class discussion to lecturing, and I have tried to carry over these preferences even when I have taught large classes in large state universities.

My education and my experience in college teaching have also affected my approach to mentoring. Mentoring the great many doctoral students with whom I have worked over the years, I have felt it important to try to get these students to drop professional attitudes in favor of getting back to the threads of personal meaning that they had originally, to deal with issues rather than just statistics, to discover meaningful problems, and to find the unique methods that are suited to those problems rather than starting with some omnicompetent methodology that they apply to every problem.

From my work with such students I learned that not only were frequent meetings together necessary but also a respect on the part of the mentor for the unconscious processes at work in the person I am mentoring so that artificial time lines and demands not interfere with the organic growth at work in the student. I have also learned that I ought not expect my doctoral students to take the risks that I have taken in my career. I have found these approaches fruitful in a variety of academic programs and institutions, and I have recommended them to other mentors in my writings.

I want to conclude this chapter with two examples, out of many, of how my mentoring helped doctoral students find a new direction not only in education but also in life. The first is a remarkable student who received his doctorate in my Religion and Literature program at Temple University in 1972. When he first thought of a dissertation topic, he came to me and said that some doctoral students in English had suggested something to him that had not been worked on before. "You ought not think in those terms," I said to him. "You ought to find a dissertation topic that means a great deal to you personally." He took my advice and wrote a brilliant doctoral dissertation on T. S. Eliot's great poem *Four Quartets*. In a separate short presentation he illustrated each quartet with photographs of the place in which it was set and played as an accompaniment music from Beethoven's last quartets. His dissertation was so good that I though it should be published though the University of Chicago Press did not agree. Many years later this same student, having gone from a deep immersion in Hinduism to Catholicism, not only wrote a profound and brilliant book on T. S. Eliot's poetry as a whole but also, to my great surprise, became totally committed to the philosophy of Martin Buber, some of which I taught him at Temple University without ever expecting him to make this a major direction in his own life as he did a quarter of a century later! One of his former students gave an anonymous grant of $100,000 for him to write a book that would make Martin Buber's classic book *I and Thou* accessible to a great many people.

At this person's request I wrote a foreword to this book that has now been published by the Paulist Press.

My second example comes from only a few years after the first. In my position as Core Faculty of the California School of Professional Psychology--San Diego, as I stated above, I established a non-statistical doctoral dissertation track. In connection with this track I held a weekly workshop in methodology supplemented by weekly individual meetings between each of the students and me. One of these students who already had an M.A. in Psychology from Duquesne University in Pittsburgh, where he had read my book *Martin Buber: The Life of Dialogue*, found himself in a quandary as to what direction to pursue in his dissertation. By listening to him and allowing him to play out these uncertainties over several weeks, rather than imposing a deadline on him, I helped him work through his hang-ups until he reached the clear decision that he wished to write his dissertation on the work of the American psychologist Abraham Maslow. This was a phenomenological dissertation of which his chapter on methodology became a model for successive generations of CSPP students (so much so indeed that one such student almost lost his doctoral degree; and with it his vocation as psychologist when it was discovered by chance that he had plagiarized the methodology chapter of my student's dissertation!). A few years later when I was asked to supply an example of mentor and protoge for a student who was doing a doctoral dissertation for another institution, I chose my experience with this student.

Then, as happened with the religion and literature doctoral student from Temple University, this student developed an interest in Buber—for psychological rather than philosophical or literary purposes. He joined me as Co-director of the Institute for Dialogical Psychotherapy that spanned a dozen years in the 1980s and 1990s. Like me, he taught one of the three seminars in our training program. His book on dialogical psychotherapy profited from his years of clinical experience and his exceptionally clear thinking and writing and has become one of the standard books in this field.

As I said above, I could adduce many other examples of changes of personal life direction that came about through the mentoring relationship between a doctoral student and myself . It may be more profitable, however, to conclude this chapter with two other examples, one of which was ambiguous in its results and another of which was, at first glance, negative in its results.

As a part of my teaching at Pendle Hill, the Quaker study center outside of Philadelphia, I gave a course in the tales of the Hasidim— the popular communal Jewish mystics of Eastern Europe during the eighteenth and nineteenth centuries to which I referred above. I taught this course with Eugenia Friedman, to whom I was married for twenty=seven years. Together we would ask students in the course to bring to class a tale that spoke to his or her condition, to use a Quaker phrase. One student in this entirely non-academic course was also my advisee. He had confided in me the long journey that he had made from almost becoming a concert pianist to almost joining an Episcopalian monastery in Liberia to wanting to work with the great French philosopher Paul Ricoeur in Paris. These vacillations from one life-d8irection to another were cut short by the sickness of his mother, which brought him back to his home in the Middle West. Now he was married and had a son. Yet he spoke of being about to desert wife and son and go off on his own.

The tale that this Pendle Hill student brought to class was "True Sorrow and True Joy." The tale concludes with the statement that true joy is like that of a man whose house has burned down and who builds it back stone by stone "and over every stone his heart rejoices." When my advisee read this story to the class, I knew at once, even before he gave his personal response to it, that his life would no longer be a meaningless circling but a straight path—that, without being able to name what it was, he had found a personal life direction.

Later this student enrolled in my doctoral program in Religion and Literature at Temple University. He was an excellent graduate student who wrote a brilliant dissertation on Martin Buber and the great French writer Albert Camus. I was very much amused at one point when he read an article by Claude Levi-Strauss in the *New York Times Magazine* that explained that existentialism, such as my student was immersing himself in, in was passé and that the "structuralism" that he himself put forward was the "real thing." For a little while this article shook my student in his resolution to complete his dissertation, but I persuaded him that one does not really find what is one's true, life direction by reading what was the latest *au courant* fad!

This student found a position in a distinguished Midwestern university and did some very creditable research and writing. I call this example ambiguous because somewhere in the midst of his academic career he decided to become an Episcopalian priest. He left his family and the university and went up to work with the Indians in northern Canada. When I was brought for a week to lecture at the University of Winnipeg, I discovered to my amazement that my student's son, whom I had known as a two-year-old, was a graduate student in philosophy at this university. When we spent some time together alone, he told me that his father had died the previous December. I told his son the story of the Hasidic tale that his father had brought to class and that so struck me at Pendle Hill. His son told me that as he lay dying in a delirium his father spoke of the house burning!

My final example seems at first glance to be negative. Shortly after I began my master's work in English at Ohio State University I met my future wife Eugenia who at the age of twenty-three had already completed all her course work for her doctorate in English. She told her advisor that she would like to write a doctoral dissertation applying Soren Kierkegaard's theory of tragedy to Shakespeare's great play *Hamlet*. "Who ever heard of applying to Shakespeare someone who lived four centuries after Shakespeare ?!" exclaimed her faculty advisor who had never read Kierkegaard. "You have to apply Aristotle who lived nineteen centuries before Shakespeare."

This response so discouraged Eugenia that she dropped out of her doctoral program in English entirely. When we moved to New York City in the fall of 1951 so that I might teach at Sarah Lawrence College, I asked Eugenia on one Saturday to take to Martin Buber (who had come to America for the first time) a lecture of his that I had just translated for him from German to English. "Professor Buber will not be able to talk with you," I said to Eugenia who had not yet met him. "He has to leave for a lecture in Cleveland in half an hour." But when Eugenia gave my translation to Martin Buber, he asked her what she was doing in life. Eugenia told him that she was trying to find a position in New York City as an editor. "Forgive me," he laughed, "but I do not see you as an editor at all. Rather I see you as working with young children." When Eugenia came back to our apartment in Riverdale and told me of her meeting with Martin Buber, I revealed to her that I had just sent off for a catalogue from Teacher's College at Columbia University because I was so impressed by the work she had done in a play school at the University of Chicago the previous summer!

Although she received two offers of editorial positions the following week, Eugenia entirely gave up her interest in becoming an editor and enrolled in Teacher's College where she received a second M.A., this one in early childhood education. Working in a number of nursery schools, Eugenia became a great nursery school teacher. Later, through my initiative, Eugenia became a teacher of modern poetry at Pendle Hill. In this field too she became a great teacher. Every year for thirty years she has been invited back to Pendle Hill to teach modern poetry, each time making the trip from San Diego to Philadelphia..

I call this a *seemingly* negative example. If her professor at Ohio State University had appreciated the really remarkable insight that Eugenia had about applying Kierkegaard to Hamlet, which others have in fact done since, she would have finished her doctorate in English at Ohio State and would undoubtedly have become a first-rater professor of English teaching and doing research at some university. But I believe that the personal life direction that she has followed instead of this has been a truly creative and meaningful one in ways that a more ordinary academic career might not have been.

It should be clear from all the above examples that I am not equating one's personal life direction with one's career although in some or perhaps many cases the two may overlap or even coincide. It should also be clear that I am not offering these examples as models for any of my readers to try to follow. As I wrote above, I have not expected, far less demanded, of my students that they should take the sort of risks that I did. We live now in a radically different time and situation than the experiences that I have discussed in this chapter.

What is more, I believe strongly that each personal life direction is unique. It may be inspired by the personal direction of another. "Lives of great men still remind us/ We can make our lives sublime," wrote the nineteenth century American poet Henry Wadsworth Longfellow, "And departing leave behind us/ Footprints on the sands of time." But we cannot simply imitate someone else's personal life direction. Once a Hasidic rabbi inherited a congregation from his father. When some of his congregants came to him and complained that in certain respects he varied from his father's rituals and teachings, he countered, "I do exactly as my father did. He did not imitate, and I do not imitate!"

CHAPTER 7

The Learning Community

Real Education Demands Real Listening

In order to have real contact with one another, we must overcome our "education"; for we are programmed to "hear" in such a way that we rarely really hear. Most of our education is an education in the methods of abstracting. Consequently, we do not hear the person who speaks but only his "opinion" or "point of view." We put him into this or that category— a "phenomenologist," an "existentialist," a "realist," a "pragmatist," a "linguistic analyst," a "structuralist" or a "deconstructionist" — and this putting into categories we call being educated. The sad thing is that so much of our sharing is pseudo-sharing because we lift it to a plane of objective discourse.

We think we communicate when we set ourselves aside as persons, agree on definitions, and meet on the high plane of abstractions. But this is really only another form of subjectivism since only a few people, if any, will agree with our terms and what we propose that they should mean. For the rest, most of what we call communication is simply mismeeting and misunderstanding people using words in different ways and not even caring enough to ask the other person what she means by what she says. Listen to the back and forth in any discussion of politics, religion, or any similar subject, and you will see what I mean.

Real listening is the exception not the rule.

A social psychologist from a department of psychology cannot really talk with a social psychologist from a department of sociology, not only because they use different terms but also because of the difference in context. But this is also true of professors from the same department. The chairman of a department of philosophy at a state university once remarked to me that at philosophy conferences the philosophers listen to one another's papers only long enough to put the speaker in some familiar category or rubric, which means they don't really listen at all.

Education as Dialogue

The student grows through her encounter with the person of the teacher and the voice of the writer. This means that no real learning takes place unless the student participates, but it also means that the student must encounter something really "other" than herself before she can learn. To most people it seems self-evident that the academic task is an affair of monologue or at most of dialectic —the interplay of points of view within a single mind or between minds minus the persons that contain those minds. Education as true dialogue must involve real contact between persons (student and student as well as student and teacher) and bring to light knowledge that is itself a product of this mutual contact.

Following the distinguished biologist and philosopher Michael Polanyi, I would define the academic task as "personal knowledge." This personal knowing is an act of commitment, a part of our calling that includes the historical setting and culture in which we have grown up as a point of departure. But we must not be imprisoned in this setting if we are to truly embrace others whose historical setting and culture may be different from our own. To the extent that we can meet in a mutual exchange that allows place for the uniqueness of our life experiences, we are growing in personal knowledge.

Such an exchange in education, whether between scientist and philosopher or anthropologist and psychologist, creates a bond of mutual trust. This leads to a committed way of learning and sharing in which the open dialogue of the scientist with the philosopher reveals what the human image is and with it what we should mean by "academic standards."

During my more than fifty years of college and university teaching I tried to promote dialogue through class discussion, breaking large classes up into small groups that reported back to the large group, seminar reports, and no examinations. This worked best in a school like Sarah Lawrence College where small classes and individual conferences with every student every week or every other week brought dialogue between teacher and student to the fore. But it was also dialogue among the students.

I once had a student who was beautiful, brilliant, and high-spirited — one who shared my concern with Quakers and pacifism and whom I counted a friend. But she did not really believe in class discussion. She could get a lot more, she argued, if I lectured instead of letting her fellow classmates talk. Once in a small seminar I let each student in turn chair the seminar instead of my always chairing it. When it came her turn, she cut the other students down ruthlessly. "You can't do that," I objected. "Yes I can. I'm the chair," she replied. "I'm still chairman pro tem," I protested. I reflected on this incident later and realized that her lack of faith in what the other students gave came from her single-minded interest in herself and what I had to say. She dismissed the unique insights and rich mutual class experiences that her classmates produced. While she and I shared many interests and ideas, we did not share the faith I had in the dialogue among the students.

Perhaps that individualism, of which she was an extreme example, accounted for the feeling I often had at the end of a class year at Sarah Lawrence College(The courses were a year long for the most part.) that this small group was unique and would never exist again. I imagined that few of the students shared my feeling because they could always count on seeing their classmates the following year (if they were not graduating) and, if they wanted to, seeing me too. But the communal reality of that particular group —the partnership of existence we shared as members of the group--would not exist again. The same is often true of temporary groups, such as weekend workshops and retreats, when they share at a deep level. The impact they make on participants can be life changing.

The Learning Community is True Community

To the extent that climates of trust and confirmation are made possible by the educational structures and the persons working within those structures, the learning community is, quite simply, the genuine community. Genuine community calls forth the uniqueness of each of its members. While this is the essence of *all* true community, it is the very heart of the learning community.

We shall understand learning better if we go back to the root meaning of the term educating—the Latin *"educe."* Education is educing. The scientific method is made up of a combination of deduction, in which one applies a general thesis to particulars, and induction, in which one goes from particulars to a general thesis. But Socrates used neither deduction nor induction; he used eduction. He educed, he led out. He started in the middle of the situation and mostly, if you follow Plato's *Dialogues* carefully, that is also where he ended, or at least it is where his hearers ended. This has very serious consequences. If educing means leading out of, it means starting with the situation where you are — not just pulling out something that is already in there, but evoking, calling forth.

The Funnel versus the Pump

Martin Buber characterizes the "old" way of looking at education by the metaphor of the funnel. The student's head is empty, you bore a hole in it and pour into it whatever you want to. The metaphor for "new" education, Buber suggests, is the pump. Progressive education, which was all the rage in the 1920's in Germany and became the rage in America some years later, was like the pump. Everything was already in the child. All one needed was to pump it out, or, to change the metaphor, the teacher watered the plant, pruned the leaves, kept off insects, i.e., facilitated the unfolding of the powers of the child.

The funnel approach is the educational philosophy of Robert Hutchins and the "Great Books." There are certain great books that the teacher teaches the student to analyze, and through that they become educated persons. The pump approach was the philosophy of John Dewey that had such a powerful influence on educational thinking in America. Dewey talked about the potentialities of students and what they needed to develop them. The new educational model is collaborative learning. The teacher facilitates the interaction between students as they learn to think, share and solve problems. Students are viewed as having something to contribute and teachers are encouraged to help the student find and offer this contribution to the group.

I taught for fourteen years at Sarah Lawrence College, which was developed in the late 1920's under the impact of the John Dewey type of progressive approach to education. We used to say, "We don't teach material. We teach the student." There is something to that, of course, but it leads at times to an approach to education that emphasizes only one side of the dialogue.

Sometimes there is a mistaken assumption that an ideal harmony exists between a teacher and her students. Often at Sarah Lawrence, there was a mutual desire on the part of the teacher and student to explore innovative learning. But Sarah Lawrence women who dated men from Columbia, Yale, and Princeton sometimes felt that their boyfriends' courses were better, even though they were more traditional ones. In the years since I left Sarah Lawrence, the traditional system of evaluating the student by a paragraph has been replaced by grades, at the request of the students! The ideal harmony between what the teacher wanted and what the student wanted did not hold. This is partly influenced by the fact that education is a means to an end in today's world. It is seen as career preparation and not as personal development. Very few people go to college to experience the latter.

Between the Funnel and the Pump

A fatal inner-outer, subjective-objective split accompanies these contrasting approaches to education. The funnel side assumes that the student is there as a mere receiver of knowledge while the pump side assumes that the teacher is merely the facilitator to bring out what is already there and needs only be unfolded. Speaking to a group of progressive world educators in Heidelberg in 1925, Buber suggested that there is a third approach. This third approach has to do with learning as dialogue, and by dialogue Buber did not mean simply Socratic dialogue. He meant people really being present one to the other. The true opposite of compulsory education is not freedom, Buber claimed, but communion.

The meaning of what you take up between you and someone else is found in the meeting itself. Is meaning merely subjective then? I don't think so. For years, I asked my students to keep a "personal-academic journal" in place of an examination. I did this because I felt it was a real way of promoting dialogue between the student, the text, and me. This journal has four steps. The first is for the student to select from the reading or the class discussion something that strikes him or her and to write it down in the journal. Step two is to try then to put it into one's own words. This means more than translating the subject into familiar categories or constructs. It means trying to go imaginatively over to where the other person is and to sense where that person is speaking from, be it author, lecturer, or fellow classmate. Step three is coming back to one's own side and responding — both intellectually and emotionally — from where one is. Step four is to relate what one is commenting on to ongoing issues of the course.

Genuine learning is an event. Simply being bombarded all the time with information does not mean that real learning takes place. Real learning is deliberate. Most true learning in our day is not a matter of taking in more but of taking in less--of focusing, of letting something come to us. The teacher, for her part, must effectively select some of what the student needs. We might well ask, "How does she know what to select?" The teacher educates herself through discovering what the student needs. How does she then discover what the student needs? Through dialogue and "inclusion" -not *asking* the student what he or she needs but experiencing the other side, imagining the real. The pupil has something that no one else in the world, including the teacher, has — a unique experience. To discover that, the teacher must ask *real* questions and not just Socratic ones.

With the proliferation of the Internet as a communication tool, teachers will have a powerful opportunity to foster genuine learning through dialogue in a way that has not been possible before. Teachers can enter the world of their students while standing their ground as educators. Students, in turn, have access to academies all over the world (including group interaction) without having to leave their homes.

What Injures the Learning Community?

Hearing and responding to one another is the simplest prerequisite of the learning community. There is no structure that can guarantee that this simple prerequisite will be met at all times. There are many structures within education that, by virtue of the complexity and competition they create, tend to get in the way. Meeting this prerequisite requires people who are in some way there for one another-- not doing the same thing but also not simply each going his or her own way. This means caring enough to have an interchange, verbal or nonverbal, caring enough to share. Our society is so competitive and polarized that people cannot hear one another. A meeting is not thought to be productive unless we can put what other people say into our own categories and then cut them down on that basis.

We are willfully mishearing others because we view their otherness as threatening to our grade, class standing, future potential or career. The prophet Amos said, "There will come a famine not of bread or water but of thirst for the words of the living God." We go over from not listening to the place where we can no longer really hear what someone else is saying even when we are hungry for relationship.

The "Climate of Trust"

One of the obvious problems of structure is size--classes of two thousand, universities of 30-, 40-, and 50,000. Yet size alone does not prevent learning from taking place. There are possibilities for learning even in the largest university if one can create within those structures a "climate of trust." Sometimes that has indeed happened. There are, of course, *limits* to creating climates of trust in situations where the larger climate is one of mistrust.

Every graduate school with which I have been associated has seemed to me to produce an unnecessary amount of anxiety for its students, who are already anxious enough by virtue of their pressured and demanding situation. This additional anxiety is created by bureaucracy and by professors in the department who are concerned with *their* reputation, *their* discipline, *their* methodology.

But some schools go far beyond that to an active mistrust of the students such that it is selfevident that any faculty member who is an "advocate" of the students is an enemy of the administration. If you want to change a structure you may, at times, have to create a whole new structure — if you can! We have to live in structures, and we have to decide when we can fight to change them, when we shall leave them, and when we must try to create new ones. In the process we discover what strengths and resources we have.

Caring for All "Points of View"

Wherever there is more than one person there is more than one point of view. By "point of view" I do not mean opinion or idea but that the other person has another touch from the regions of existence, another soil, another faith. Each person brings something quite concrete and unique into the relationship. If that is not recognized, it is usually the fault of *all* the persons involved. There tends to be an implicit contract through which one or more persons allow themselves to be dominated.

When I was in high school we were often given "opinion polls." But opinions are not really significant. They only reveal the surface of a person's mind — and often not even that when the person wishes to deceive others or even themselves. A point of view, as I am using that phrase here, is a deeply held attitude that comes from the depths of one's being.

The Fear that Difference Will Lead to Conflict

One of the reasons that we have communities of affinity is that we are so afraid of difference, of conflict, of otherness that we imagine if we admit any, we shall kill each other down to the last person. Some time ago, the now-defunct *New York Herald Tribune* used to bring high school students every year from many countries to spend a year in America. These students would come to Sarah Lawrence College for a week's workshop before separating to attend high school in cities throughout the United States. I was teaching a course in Comparative Religion at the time and was invited to conduct a workshop with these students. I accepted eagerly since I had never had contact with so many students of so many different religions all in one group.

I asked each of these students to write a short statement for me to use as a basis for discussion. The Catholic student from Africa and the Catholic student from South America wrote the identical catechism, but once we got into discussion we found that their religions were by no means identical. The atheist from Indo-China was a Buddhist; the atheist from Paris was a Sartrian existentialist. These young people loved these interchanges, and I did too. Ironically, the woman who ran the week's workshop called me up afterward and said, "I am going to take four of these students on television and try to do what you did about religion. But, of course, I am not going to allow any issues to arise"!

Specialization as an Obstacle

What gets in the way of the learning community being a true caring community? Size, structure, program boxes, mistrust, lack of real communication, concern with public relations, *and* the specialization through which professors know more and more about less and less. There is no learning community, no caring community, if we use our language games in such a way that they shut out people who do not use our language. This is extremely pervasive. Disciplines and departments are good, but they are not ends in themselves. The problem with specialization arises when it is no longer content to be a useful tool and claims instead to be the only real province of knowledge. As soon as one says that there is only one right language, then the learning community is endangered — not by specialization *per se* but by allowing it to become a dogma, a shibboleth.

David Hume said that if a book has anything in it but reasoning and matters of numbers it should be cast into the fire. We see the same attitude in the modern logical positivist who says that literature, religion and most philosophy do not mean anything. Or the linguistic analyst who reduces every statement of values to personal preference — "This is what I like. I wish you would like the same." — so that there is no referent beyond oneself. This adds to the mutual mistrust. Instead of trying to understand why a person says what she or he says, one is already seeing through and unmasking that person in advance. Post-modern deconstructionism often seems to be trying to carry this unmasking *ad absurdum*.

Genuine community is not an ideal that any one community of specialists can claim. It is a direction in which we are trying to move, a reality that we are trying to build in every situation in which we find ourselves. I would question in the most serious fashion whether anything worthy of the name of learning is going on if there is not this dialogue that is open to otherness — not just in the sense that you may say your piece and I will say my piece, or that our competing presences keep each of us driven toward greater achievement but in the sense that we grow together even in opposing each other, even in conflict, because we really are coming up against each other.

The Meaning of Presentness in the Learning Community

Heraclitus of Ephesus spoke of his fellow Ephesians as being "present yet absent." What teacher has not had that experience with his or her students?! Presentness is not a thing. It is a presence with and toward others. The French Catholic existentialist philosopher Gabriel Marcel speaks of being with someone else who robs you of your own sense of presence through the way he or she is removed and detached.

Presentness is a reality that happens between persons. What threatens this presence in learning is the tendency to divide thought from feeling so that we may imagine we are present if our thought is there even though our feelings are quite repressed. Not so long ago people turned that upside down and said that the only important thing is to have feelings — "gut level hostility" — and the rest is meaningless. Presentness means being present with our whole being as we are at that moment. It means not withholding ourselves, but it does not mean saying everything that comes to mind. One way of not withholding ourselves is to have the courage to respond.

A curious form of absence that I have often seen is where people ask questions, putting the question forward but hiding themselves in the background. Once at a lecture, a man whose face was deeply etched by the encounter with life asked a question about evil. After I had answered it, I said to him, "Perhaps you would like to say something from your experience." "Oh, I've never had any experience of evil," he replied. He was withholding himself, probably without being consciously aware that he was doing so.

The Limits of the Learning Community

We discover the limits of the learning community in the concrete situation. In classes that most students take only because they fulfill a requirement, it is hard for true learning to take place, no matter how good the teacher may be. But even where the students are genuinely interested, they are often inhibited from taking part in class discussion by the fact that students are rewarded for being articulate. The students who are more facile with words than others get the best grades.

Schools ought to be places where students experiment and make mistakes. Instead they are all too often places where students are afraid to speak up for fear that what they say will not sound smooth and finished to the teacher or even to their fellow classmates. I noticed this particularly forcibly when a transfer student joined a class I taught at Sarah Lawrence College. She was intelligent, but she did not have the verbal facility of the other students and was looked down on for it.

For years I wondered why it was that students would put their hands up and then invariably begin their comment or question by saying, "No." I finally concluded that that "No" was a disclaimer, a denial, something that made it safe to go ahead.

CHAPTER 8

The Healing Community

"The authentic assurance of duration arises in the fact of the growth and rise of being into Thou, that the holy primary word makes itself heard in them all. Thus the time of human life is shaped into a fullness of reality, and even though human life neither can nor ought to overcome the connexion with *It*, it is so penetrated with relation that relation wins in it a shining, streaming constancy: the moments of meeting are then not flashes in the dark but like the rising moon in a clear, starlit night . . . . It is not the periphery, the community that comes first but the common quality of relation to the Centre. This alone guarantees the authentic existence of the community"

Only when these two arise—the binding up of time in a relational life of [redemption] and the binding up of space in the Community that is made one by its Centre . . . does there exist . . . a world that is house and home, a dwelling for man in the universe.

Martin Buber, *I and Thou*

I have seen that community and a close relation with the land can enrich human life beyond all comparison with material wealth and technological sophistication.

Helena Norbert-Hodge, *Ancient Futures*

During the year and a half in which I worked at the "Institute for the Feeble Minded" as part of the three and a half years of Civilian: Public Service I performed as a conscientious objector during the Second World War I became a thorough-going mystic spending three hours every day in meditation and trying during working to hours to "recollect" my mind through repeating a Hindu mantram. I would not associate with any other members of our unit, associating only with three other mystically-minded members of our Gemeinde..

Toward the end of that time, however, I read and was entranced by Martin Buber/x early book *The Legend of the Baal-Shem*, ,the Baal Shem Tov (Good Master of the Name [of God}, Israel ben Eliezer (1700-1760 being the founder of the communal Jewish mysticism of East European Jewry known as Hasidism. . As a resiltl I gradually traded in my immersion in Christian and Buddhist mysticism and after that the Hindu Vedanta, all of which seemed to me in retroso;ect toh isolated and self- and world-denying, for the communal mysticism of joy and life-affirmation that I found in Hasidism. I was not, however,, able to join any group of contemporary Hasidim, whom I found to be what I have called above a "community of like-mindedness, or affinity' in contrast to what I saw as the openness of the original Hasidim. Nor was I able to join any commune.

Instead, influenced by the powerful but for me personally disastrous amateur psychodramatic group in which I took part during my last months of Civilian Public Service (I narrate my whole experience in Civilian: Public Service and describe my participation in the amateur psychodrama in detail in my still unpublished memoir, : *'Down in My Heart- Part II: The Group Dance'*—all in novel form.) I have spent almost forty years concerned with individual, group,, and, through my friend the late Ivan Boszormenyi-Nagy "Contextual [intergenerational family] Therapy. In addition to being the author of two books and many articles on psychotherapy, I practiced psychotherapy for more than a quarter of a century and was for fifteen years Co-Director of the Institute of Dialogical Psychotherapy and teacher in its two-year training program.

Nonetheless, in unfolding Martin Buber's conception of the "normative limitation" of psychotherapy, I have pointed out in my book *The Healing Dialogue in Psychotherapy* that, while there cannot be mutuality of "inclusion or imagining the real between therapist and client slnce only the thera;ist can ex;erience both sides of the client-therapist relationship, there is mutuality of trust, and mutuality of concern between therapist and client since the therapist is concerned not only for his or her individual "patient" but also for the sick family and the sick community from which the client comes.

It was only after thinking I had completed this book on *Foundations of True Community* that it occurred to me that I ought to turn my concern for the sick community around and add a chapter on "The Healing Community" Although I did not use this expression, I had something of the sort in mind when my1983 book *The Confirmation of Otherness: In Family, Community,. and Society* was published)..

By "the healing community" I do not mean any sort of psychiatric lnstitution but true community itself. My wife Aleene points out that on the cul de sac on which we live,such a true community exists—not indeed in the fact that we have a block party every Labor Day or even that it is a cul de sac but that in the twenty-seven years in which we have both lived in this house, we have witnessed genuine community grow and sustain itself while children have grown up and gone away to college and to work. Every genuine community is a healing community, for it is this above all that we need for the necessary healing to take place, and it is this that must be the true foundation of that dialogical psychotherapy with which I have been concerned for so many years.

Having equated healing community with genuine community, I might adduce a myriad of examples if I had knowledge of all the genuine communities that exist in America, Israel, and many other countries. I wish here, however, to give as example only one healing community of which I know personally. This is the community that the reverend Dr. Willy Crespo has built in the federal jjail in San Diego over the past thirty years. I became acquainted with Rev. Crespo originally as one of the trainees in the training program of our Institute of Dialogical Psychotherapy.

Building Community in Prison

Through the two-year training program of our Institute for Dialogical Psychotherapy of which I was Co-Director during the fifteen to twenty years of its existence, I came to know Wilfredo Crespo. This involved several visits to the prison where he has worked for more than a quarter of a century both as chaplain and as counselor. During our last visit, my wife Aleene and I met with a select group of prisoners who had volunteered to be in a learning program with Rev. Crespo. We were deeply impressed by the presence and participation of the prisoners that we met with and the totally non-authoritarian leadership that Rev. Wilfredo Crespo provided. Here, in a federal prison—the most unlikely place imaginable—we found real community and real caring,

To appreciate adequately Dr. Crespo's remarkable and, so far as I know, unique achievement in working in the prison in which he is both counselor and chaplain, we must look first at his description of the difficulties that he faced in trying to build community. We cannot do better than read Rev. Crespo's own assessment of the problems he has faced in in trying to build community during a quarter of a century of work with the inmates in his Metropolitan Correctional Center:

We have about 20,000 inmates coming in and out of the institution every year, creating a tremendous amount of movement, wear and tear on the building, and putting extra demands on staff. In this chaotic atmosphere inmates grapple with loss, fear, tension, and an uncertain future.

Programs offered to the inmates population often **look** better on paper than they actually are. Some reasons for this include high turn over of the inmates—they may start a program but never finish it--, many materials are not translated into Spanish for the Spanish-speaking population, staff get burnt out;, and since staff often gets called on for other things, they end up simply giving the inmates a video to watch or a handout to read. The programs lack continuity, consistency, and integrity.

Basically programs have been limited to religious services and GED classes for inmates wishing to complete their high school equivalency. . . We offer programs for every religion present in our institution throughout the week and evenings. While I have been at the MCC, I developed a 40-hour drug program that focuses on the nature and effects of various kinds of drugs and their impact on health, family and society. I started AA and NA programs, anger management groups, abuse groups, meditation groups, poetry groups, and women's groups, men's bible groups, and critical bible groups, Spanish men's culture groups, and around 2002 [my wife] Maria and I started a Socratic [Dialogue] group.

The intellectual atmosphere in the MCC, and I suspect in other prisons, is generally quite limited. The quality of books available in our libraries leaves much to be desired in terms of intellectual stimulation. There is an overbearing atmosphere in the jail, one that corrodes, deadens and destroys the inmates' ability to think clearly, critically and responsibly. In prisons and jails base instincts surface and rule through sex, color, race, and power. Prison is not a place where trust easily develops, nor is it a place where inquiry of ideas is possible without fear or threat. In fact, prison is a place where oue learns to play along in whatever way the officials expect you to and to keep both your feelings and your thoughts to yourself. Prison has never been a places where inmates take responsibility; in fact, it is a breeding ground for ...training in becoming a victim of the system and a fertile ground for disavowing one's responsibility for one's own life. In a relatively short time inmates learn the psychological language that will get them medications for depression and/or anxiety while earning for themselves a diagnosis that will follow them the rest of their lives.[6]

One of Rev. Crespo's stated aims is to provide a context for community development through which inmates can ask significant questions and wrestle reality with others. He sees his Metropolitan Correctional Center as *"working on zero ground, sacred ground."* Recognizing that the prison is the place where lives are crushed and hopefully renewed, he wishes to provide a solid context for the experience of a real community. Through the men's groups and the Socratic dialogues that he conducts, he promotes trust and community growth among the inmates. In doing this he recognizes the importance of himself as change agent and leader as a role model for creative and developing community in the jail and an example for inmates who wish to mirror its qualities after they have left jail.

Because a majority of the inmates have less than a high school education and mental difficulties in addition, Bible study and group meetings become an important door for experiencing healing and releasing pent-up emotions. Another door is the bar song groups in which the inmates and Rev. Crespo with them sing songs of remembrance, love, and loss that melt the walls between them.

In order to create a ministry specific to jails, Rev. Crespo trains volunteers to understand how to use body language, personal space and intermittent eye contact as vital skills. "During the small group process inmates learn and practice 'boundary function,' experience inter/intra group discussions about sensitive issues of faith and life." Rev. Crespo says of the work that he has done in prisons for 32 years, "I really put myself out there and do everything I can to touch with humanity what I consider to be one of the most difficult populations." I venture that what he does is unique. It is certainly not a technique that can be objectively applied in other situations. Describing his goals, he says that he really would like to know whether the inmates he works with experience community and are moved by the humanity of another.[7]

"The chaplain," writes Wilfredo Crespo in his doctoral dissertation for Seabury-Western Theological Seminary, "by engaging inmates one-on-one becomes pivotal in creating a 'real religious community.'" Dr. Crespo points to doors that only the inmates themselves can open through discovering how they interpret loss, shame, and guilt and wrestle with life in search of personal direction. The chaplain can create a context of trust in prison and offer inmates their first relationship in which truth and forgiveness are combined. "The chaplain/inmate relationship is one door where the inmate rediscovers himself and receives, as by grace, healing, redirection, and renewed faith and hope." In addition, singing songs together creates a context in which it is safe for inmates to connect with others.

The Men's Group, which meets on alternate weeks with the Socratic dialogue group, brings inmates together in the chapel to discuss books and articles that could stimulate them to experience community. Creating awareness of the self in relation to others, the Men's Group provides inmates with a sense of a larger reality. Along with the Socratic group, it engages inmates in a dialogue where they can begin to experience trust, start being truthful, and learning to be open. Through being honest and open about the ambiguities of life and faith, the chaplain can steer clear of that attitude of certainty that becomes an invitation for the inmates to play the religious game and live superficially in prison.

In the conclusion of his dissertation Rev. Dr. Crespo makes a beautiful statement about the aim of the methods that he uses:
Every interaction with inmates, every crisis and even the smallest details of daily life in prison can be used as an opportunity or door through which I attempt to engage and wrestle with the inmate for an authentic meeting. I believe that with an authentic meeting a door opens to both of us to help us see each other as mutual , [a door] where honest discussion can begin about deep questions, pain and the uncertainty of how to respond.

CHAPTER 9

Overcoming Bias

A Direction of Movement

Like everything else that we have discussed in this book, the "unbiased community" is a direction of movement rather than an ideal or even a blueprint. This is important in an age where more and more people in public service, education, health care, and the popular media are talking about community building. Within many circles, bias is thought to be a roadblock to true community. For example, education trains teachers to be sensitive to their cultural biases in hopes of raising their awareness of how biases in the classroom can undermine a child's efforts to learn. Likewise, the health care industry strives to reeducate its professionals to be more sensitive to biases that may interfere with certain individual's ability to obtain a proper diagnosis, treatment or intervention. It's fair to say that since the late 1960's, the United States has moved in the direction of eliminating biases that might discriminate against someone for being black, female, gay, disabled or otherwise subject to unfair treatment. The Civil Rights Movement, the Women's Movement, the Gay Rights Movement, to name a few, have all helped raise our social consciousness about the evils of bias within communities be they large or small.

With all of the strides we have made toward becoming a nation that supports equality, fairness, and civil rights, we have to ask why we are still confronted with issues that let us know how far we still must go? Why do women still make less money than men when given the same job with the same level of skill, experience and education? Why are blacks, Hispanics, Asians and other ethnic groups still the target of hatred, discrimination and racial stereotyping? Why do people turn a blind eye to gay bashing until something so heinous occurs that we can no longer ignore the problem? Why do neo-Nazi groups still have strongholds of support in communities that claim to love God and neighbor?

We might conclude that there is a serious schism between the ideals we espouse and the manner in which we rationalize our social obligations to neighbor, stranger and alien. This is nothing new. Historical timelines are littered with the bodies of those who died at the hand of someone else's cruelty, apathy or indifference. Bias in its most benign form reduces someone else's "thou" to an "it," that opens the way for mismeeting, disconfirmation, and antipathy. How, we ask ourselves, might we resist biases that undermine or malign the partnership of existence?

We have seen that communities of affinity believe that tolerating differences will weaken them or rob them of their ground while communities that confirm otherness view differences among their members as essential to their vitality. The basic distinction that we have made between these two types of community — that of affinity, or like-mindedness, and that which confirms the otherness of its members and of those in other communities — is already implicitly a distinction between a biased community and one that is not. It is the community of affinity, or like-mindedness, that gives rise to the "we-they " mentality that turns those outside the community into strangers, aliens, or all too often enemies. It is the "we-they" mentality that from of old has again and again polarized communities against one another and against the minorities whose life stance is different from their own.

In distinguishing between the "community of affinity," or "like-mindedness" and the "genuine community" that confirms otherness, we have already cast light on the chief source of bias in community—the tendency of communities to marginalize those they perceive as threatening by virtue of their differences. This tendency is so strong that one might well ask whether the very existence of community and of the security it gives to its adherents makes movement in the direction of an unbiased community unthinkable.

The contention of this book is that it is not unthinkable if it is looked at in its concrete embodiments. For much of the marginalizing that takes place is based on unreal fear and hysteria—fear that being open to differences will weaken the community or rob it of its ground, hysteria that arises when the adherents of community strike out at "others" rather than strengthening their own ground. Here too Buber's "meeting others and holding one's ground when one meets them" is apposite.

Since this tendency toward bias is as old as humanity itself, we have to ask what in our current situation makes it necessary for us to emphasize it. Today, as never before, there is a movement in state governments in America to deny benefits and assistance to indigent and alien members of our society. To take only one example, California's former governor Pete Wilson threw all the weight of his office into denying assistance of any kind to the illegal immigrants who flocked to California from the Latin Americas. The growing number of homeless and indigent on the streets of the great cities of America suggests that we may not be too far behind such disaster areas as Mexico City, Cairo, and Calcutta.

A second form of marginalizing that we see today is the continued refusal of the Catholic Church to ordain women as priests. While this might seem at first glance to be only the concern of the Catholics themselves, we cannot help seeing it as a glaring example of the second-class citizenship of women that still holds in many areas of the world. When I was visiting professor at Hebrew Union College-Jewish Institute of Religion in Cincinnati in 1956, I remember one faculty lunch when an older professor said that there was, in fact, nothing in the Jewish law against women being rabbis. Yet he thought the idea totally preposterous. In the years since women have become rabbis not only within Reform Judaism but also within Reconstructionist and Conservative congregations. Many Episcopalian churches literally split over the issue of whether women could be priests. The last pope's dead-set attitude against this happening in the Catholic Church cannot hold out forever against the desire of women to be full partners in the churches to which they belong. In this same connection we might cite the reluctance in corporate settings to promote women to positions with equal status and pay of their male counterparts. The argument against this is that women do not in fact do the same work as men and so should be paid less. But this is a circular argument since capable women have long since proved that they can do the same work.

The Community of Resistance and Hope

The community of resistance and hope is, in the words of Gustav Landauer--the great German socialist and close friend of Martin Buber--a "striving, with the help of an ideal, to create a new reality" (Gustav Landauer, "For Socialism"). In these times of monumental threats to human and global community, those who advocate a formation of a new community of human diversity and tolerance must, in the words of my author-scholar friend Toshio Whelchel, "have an ideal, a vision, a desire to move along a direction, and a path of serious hope and commitment." This path of hope, however, must not hinder the human possibility of community through a rigid and conformist blueprint.

A marker on the road to a new and true community is the fact that more and more young people, in the Americas, Europe, and Asia, are talking and taking action outside the traditional structures of modern Western capitalism. In Seattle, Washington, recently a broad coalition of environmental activists joined together with international labor and anarchist organizations to protest the global corporate domination of labor, land, and capital in the form of the World Trade Organization (WTO). This protest came at a time when such regional resistance to global domination was thought to have ended decades before. As a result the possibility of a broad coalition of active organization against global capitalism along the lines of regional and local community resistance has been brought to the fore.

The 1955-1965 Social Revolution

One of the principal roadblocks to true community has been modern industrial society's refusal to allow the full expression of basic civil and human rights on the part of those who fall outside the cultural domain of Anglo-European origin. The struggles for human and civil rights initiated by southern blacks during the 1950s represent a culmination of political and social efforts to bring about an end to legal *apartheid*--Jim Crow segregation, practiced and sanctioned as a legal and appropriate way of life in America since the 1860s. The struggle for black liberation in America represented a movement of resistance motivated by the desire to bring about a new community, a "new reality" in the midst of the oppression and debasement of black communities.

During this period of social revolution from 1955 to 1965 many members of the dominant American society looked upon the community of resistance as attempting to undermine the very fabric of American culture and society--the culture of *apartheid* and race subordination--and therefore as being subversive of the American way of life. As a result. many American political and corporate institutions have made a sustained effort to contain the dangerous potential for social change unleashed by the black resistance movement during the 1950s and 1960s.

Similarly, the struggle for Gay and Lesbian rights has remained an uphill battle against forces of conformism and heterosexual purity sanctioned and dictated by the majority of orthodox Christian, Jewish, and Muslim institutions. A current example is California Proposition 22--an anti gay and lesbian measure making illegal marriage between homosexuals (already illegal under California law) whose supporters call for its passage in order to "protect marriage"! Since then President Bush has proposed an amendment to the United States Constitution to make gay marriage illegal under federal law.

The Growth of Extremist Groups

We cannot turn our eyes in the direction of unbiased communities if we do not begin by recognizing that in America in recent years there has been an alarming growth of extremist groups that flourish on the very denial of the validity of those outside the group.

In his recent book *Millennium Rage: Survivalists, White Supremacists, and the Doomsday Prophecy*, Phillip Lamy has given us an in-depth picture of just such groups. After describing the assassination of the Denver Jewish talk radio personality Alan Berg by a racist hate group called "The Silent Brotherhood," Lamy comments:

The Silent Brotherhood planned the killing of Berg out of hate for Jews and a right-wing-inspired paranoia of world domination by the Jews and minority "mud peoples"—blacks, Latinos, Asians, and the entire "polyglot" cesspool that choked America. Such beliefs run deep in our culture and form the nucleus of a white supremacist Christian survivalism—the most fanatic and vitriolic of the right wing. Those who have used the rhetoric of the millennium for personal or political gain often tend to demonize other peoples, even committing genocide in the name of religion and ideology.[8]

Lamy traces this trend back to the Ku Klux Klan and the fascism of the American Nazis in the 30s as well as to the infamous nineteenth century forgery by the Czar's police of *The Protocols of the Elders of Zion*. But it has been widely recognized since the Holocaust (the *Shoah*) [which these white supremacist groups uniformly deny ever took place] that hatred of the Jews is deeply rooted in Christianity. As Lamy himself points out, "The idea that the Antichrist would be a Jew and that the 'mysterious' Jews were his followers has been a consistent belief in Christianity, though marginal to mainstream theology, for centuries."[9] The farm crisis, unemployment, and declining standards of living provided fertile soil in the 1970s and 1980s for white supremacist groups to spread the myth of the Jewish conspiracy and copies of *The Protocols* themselves across agrarian and rural areas of America. "Spewing the rhetoric of the Jewish world conspiracy as the root cause of farmers' and America's problems," some of these groups "became linked to paramilitary and survival training centers and to vigilantes, mercenaries, and the Ku Klux Klan."

The advent of computers, the internet, fax machines, and e-mail has resulted in the forging of "virtual communities" of like-minded Christian survivalists. The most unifying theology for these diverse groups is Christian Identity, "providing a common religion for survivalists, neo-Nazis, and anti-government zealots, thereby fusing religion with hate, guns, and an apocalyptic fear of the future." More recently skinheads have been added to the mix. After the scandals of the 1980s the world of "televangelism" and mass media prophecy is back as strong as ever. That these grassroots groups might grow into "an American millennial fascism" is a serious possibility, warns Lamy.[10]

In many ways the right wing revolutionaries of today seek to overthrow the gains made by the civil rights, women's, gay and lesbian, and environmental movements of the 1960s and 1970s. Should the antigovernment, anti-foreigner, anti-Semitic, and Christian supremacist values and beliefs of right wing survivalism continue to develop in American society, the potential for future Oklahoma Cities, or worse, is almost assured.[11]

In the face of all this what hope is there for "unbiased community"? Do unbiased communities have a secret that permits individuals within them to be who they are? Is it a philosophy of tolerance that governs the unbiased community or a watered down ideology that shuns standards of any kind?

There are elements in every movement, group, organization and institution that promote their ideology above everyone else's. To the extent that we can observe how an organization rationalizes and justifies bias on ideological grounds, we can say that no organization is without bias. The same is true for communities. There is no such thing as an unbiased community because an unbiased community is not an entity with fixed and reliable proportions but a direction of movement that is adjusting and readjusting in each lived moment. The unbiased community is the community that walks on the narrow ridge between two abysses --loss of boundaries and group egocentrism), and is— vulnerable time and again to falling away from the partnership of existence.

Unbiased communities cannot be identified in terms of universal values. Bias in Tulsa where I grew up is not comparable to bias at Harvard where I went to college. I can't judge Harvard's brand of tolerance to be more evolved than my home-town's simply because I like it better. Each community has its unique expression of inclusion and confirmation and therefore cannot appeal to every one at all times. Tolerance or bias cannot be measured in purely objective terms. This introduces an interesting paradox. Unbiased communities, while striving to be inclusive and dialogical, may in fact seem closed and hostile to an objective observer.

To expect an unbiased community to look or feel completely open to anyone and everyone who might choose to cross its threshold misunderstands the term "unbiased." It is not synonymous with indiscriminate. Genuine communities that confirm otherness must have a center if they are to be truly confirming. How can I confirm you if I have no genuine ground of my own from which to oppose you? It is when a community categorically and systematically refuses to tolerate or confirm someone on the basis of his race or her gender alone that discrimination becomes dangerous.

In our culture there has been no distinction made in recent times between healthy and flagrant discrimination. We intuitively understand that we must discriminate between what is and isn't acceptable in relationships every time we consider making a new friend or redefine the boundaries in a relationship we already have. But how does that transfer to the institutional settings where discrimination of any kind is thought of as bad? While observing an interview panel recently, David Damico was amazed to see how the selection process unfolded as equally qualified applicants for a social work position were disqualified on the basis of subjective and personal attitudes among the interviewers. Was David watching something sinister and discriminatory or was he witnessing the process by which we human beings make choices about relationships in the workplace? No one on the panel said, "I don't like that last person we interviewed, he was too effeminate." But members of the panel did joke and laugh about the personalities they met during the course of the morning.

Communities are a complex intertwining of relationships and activities that require members to interact on a personal level while being able to perform specialized tasks that may require certain training, education or life experience. The unbiased community must hold the tension between one's qualifications to do a particular thing that needs doing and one's eligibility to be included as a full-fledged member of the human race regardless of religion, color, sex, and lifestyle.

Bias and the Struggle for Equality

Equality and dignity cannot be won apart from a community that confirms otherness. A woman cannot claim equality and expect her claim to be validated simply because she makes a good argument for it. Even if she succeeds in changing the attitudes of all of the men who know her, she will not make equality for other women in other places a reality. One community's success in holding the tension between bias and inclusion does not guarantee success for other communities that may try to imitate or adopt the successful community's model. The advances of recent decades, as we have seen, have still not brought about the full realization of human rights and social civic dignity. In the partnership of existence people meet and confirm one another as persons while holding the tension with those things that make them different.

One woman working as a social worker for homeless people explained the difficulty she had at first. "For me growing up, people got homeless because they were lazy or uneducated. To be homeless was to be a failure. After working with homeless people, I can't imagine how I ever thought that. Sure there are people who are homeless because they have poor work habits or inadequate education, but this isn't something they are proud of. I realize now they are people just like me. We laugh at the same jokes, worry about our kids the same way and want the same kinds of things in life. Now when I hear someone talking about homeless people in categorical terms, I want to ask them, 'Who do you know that is homeless? How much time have you spent getting to know them?' How can anyone know what they really need or want without asking them?"

Equality doesn't happen when an underprivileged person or group of persons fight their way to the top and overthrow the status quo. Equality happens when those with privilege climb down from the elevated notions that make them feel separate and more secure than the rest of the world. When the social worker set out to really meet and not just manage the homeless people she'd long believed were different and inferior, she opened the way for equality and partnership.

Role-Power and Modern Community

Finally, an unbiased community is one that encourages partnership among its members on the basis of role *and* relationship. In the past, communities have made the mistake of giving their members specific roles or duties based more on the needs of the community than on the interests of the person(s) performing them. Roles in communities tend to have hierarchical outcomes over time that can harm the partnership of existence by ranking members according to the roles they play and doling out the most role-power to members with the highest rank.

A male bishop in the church has more role-power than a female deacon or teacher. Regardless of the influence her role as teacher has on the community members she impacts, her power to influence the Bishop is reduced simply because he outranks her. By setting up hierarchical roles, communities, religious and otherwise, can control the degree to which they can be affected from within. Furthermore, hierarchical communities depend as much on subordination as cooperation. Members cooperate in part by accepting the community's ranking system as incontestable.

One problem with hierarchical communities is that people are dependent upon a chain of command that becomes increasingly impersonal with each next higher level of decision-making. Confirmation no longer happens in genuine dialogue but in a complex process that may feel unfair or ambiguous to the individual seeking it. If a woman wants to change her role from teacher to priest, she is dependent on those above her to hear her petition. Even if she gets her petition heard, she may never have the chance to enter genuine dialogue with the individual who has the power to decide whether she is promoted or recognized. When a distant decision-maker with role-power says she cannot be promoted because she is a woman and therefore not eligible for ordination, she is left to feel that her devotion, education, service and sense of direction are meaningless.

Hierarchical communities are not a thing of the past. The difference between now and one or two generations ago is that individuals are more apt to challenge hierarchical systems—whether they be the military, educational institutions, the church or the American Medical Association. This has led to a siege mentality on the part of many hierarchical communities that are not ready to undergo reform.

Capitalism can be credited for threatening hierarchical models of community because, in principle, anyone ambitious enough can get to the top of the ladder and be king or queen. Whereas the bishop or general achieves rank through a lengthy and class-conscious selection process, the CEO often gets to the top of the ladder with little or no due process. This is especially true in today's exploding internet and e-mail commerce marketplace.

It is a mistake, however, to think of capitalism as being less bias-prone because some of us are able to create our own social roles. Capitalism, in and of itself, offers no genuine means to reach authentic social roles. In fact, it often pits community members against one another encouraging competition, comparison, divisiveness, rewarding drivenness and punishing timidity. By allowing individuals to buy entitlements or privileges apart from a confirming community, capitalism has been as destructive to the partnership of existence as hierarchical authoritarianism. It has created a generation of individuals whose sense of self-importance and autonomy are so over-inflated that any sense of needing to be confirmed and included in a larger community is absent.

Capitalism has been largely responsible for making genuine dialogue an absurdity to the modern mind, the partnership of existence a clunky relic to be discarded. Sadly, there are individuals in today's modern world who have achieved success in the capitalist sense but whose existence is groundless and void of genuine dialogue.

The true challenge for the unbiased community is to reconstruct a spirituality rooted and grounded in the concrete meeting between persons. "When two people really touch each other as persons," I say in my book *Touchstones of Reality*, "this touching is not merely a one-sided impact: it is a mutual revelation of life stances."

CHAPTER 10

Women and the Confirmation of Otherness

"To emancipate woman is to refuse to confine her to the relations she bears to man,,, not to deny them to her; let her have her independent existence and she will continue nonetheless to exist for him *also*: mutually recognizing each other as subject, each will yet remain for the other an *other*" wrote Simone de Beauvoir at the end of her famous book *The Second Sex* (de Beauvoir, 1971, p. 731).

Maria Lugones in her essay "Doing Theory" has an attitude toward otherness that brings her quite close to Simone de Beauvoir, Martin Buber, and myself:

Traveling to someone's "world" is a way of identifying with them because by traveling to their "world" we can understand *what it is to be them and what it is to be ourselves in their eyes*. Only when we have traveled to each other's "worlds" are we fully subjects to each other . . . . Without knowing the other's "world," one does not know the other, and without knowing the other one is really alone in the other's presence because the other is only dimly present to one. Through traveling to other people's "world" we discover that there are "worlds" in which those who are the victims of arrogant perceptions are really subjects, lively beings, resistors, constructors of visions even though in the mainstream construction they are animated only by the arrogant perceiver and are pliable, foldable, file-awayable, classifiable (Anzaldua, 1990, p. 401 f.).

Another woman of color whose ideas come quite close to my concept of the confirmation of otherness is the African-American poetess Audrey Lorde. In her book *Sister, Outsider* Lorde characterizes racism, sexism, heterosexism` and homophobia as forms of human blindness that "stem from the same root—an inability to recognize the notion of difference as a dynamic human force, one which is enriching rather than threatening to the defined self, when there are shared goals" (Lorde, 1984, p. 45). "Difference must be not merely tolerated, but seen as a fund of necessary polarities between which our creativity sparks like a dialectic. . . . .Difference is that raw and powerful connection from which our personal power is forged " (Lorde, 1984, p. 111 .

Lorde comes remarkably close to my own distinction between "the community of affinity" [or likemindedness] and "the community of otherness"[the community that confirms otherness](Friedman,1983, chap. 13): "Without community there is no liberation . . . But community must not mean a shedding of our differences, nor the pathetic pretense that these differences do not exist" (Lorde, 1984, p. 112).She applies this conviction not only to the relation of Blacks and Whites and men and women but also to the Black community itself: "A small and vocal part of the Black community lost sight of the fact that unity does not mean unanimity . . . .Unity implies the coming together of elements which are, to begin with, varied and diverse in their particular natures. Our persistence in examining the tensions within diversity encourages growth toward our common goal" (Lorde, 1984, p.136).

Rosalind Petchesky and following her Zillah Eisenstein point uut that confirming women in their otherness and humanity (my teerms) means recognizing the reproductive rights that women have and that men cannot have:

The assault on women's reproductive rights has demanded that feminists both defend and push beyond the existing boundaries of a woman's privacy and her right to choose. Our new conceptions must encompass a notion of personal privacy which is also grounded in women's collective and shared need for reproductive control of their bodies. I am indebted to Rosalind Petchesky's formulation of this need. She eloquently advises that "We must retrieve reproductive rights from the heavy baggage of liberal exclusivity with which they have been encumbered, and ground ourselves in the actual political struggles of the civil rights and feminist movements. We must develop a definition of rights "that maintains a notion of women's moral and political agency both as individuals and as members of collectives" (Petchesky, 1990, p. 395 quoted in Eisenstein, 1994, p. 197 f.).

To put her conviction into practice Rosalind Petchesky founded and for many years directed the International Organization for Women's Reproductive Rights, a research and action group active in eleven countries worldwide.

The Problematic Tension between Personal Uniqueness and Social Role

What should be the highest flowering of the human the exhilaration and exploration of what it means to be a woman in relationship to a man or to another woman or a man in relation to a woman or another man in this particular historical situation--is submerged in the confusion and distortion of the universally oppressive social role. Through this imposed social role both women and men are subject to the tyranny of both men's and women's notions of what it means to be "feminine" and to be "masculine." The battle for gender liberation is a battle for the wholeness of the human being, a battle for a woman's and a man's right to be a person.

Women's social/cultural role begins in infancy, according to the authors of *Women's Growth in Connection,* and is central in the development of the woman's self. While girls are encouraged to develop their abilities to feel as the other feels, boys are systematically diverted from it. For girls, being present with the other "mutual empathy," or what I would rather call "inclusion," is experienced as self enhancing, whereas for boys it may come to be experienced as engulfing, or threatening. In intimate relations men fear the danger of entrapment or betrayal, being smothered or humiliated by rejection and deceit. Women, in contrast, are afraid of isolation: if they stand out or are set apart by success, they fear they will be abandoned.

For girls being in relationship, sensing the feelings of the other and attending to the interaction between themselves and others, is a desirable *goal,* not a means to some other end such as one's own self development. Women have long played the role of listening to and confirming men, their children, and their friends. But when they feel, as they often do, that they do not have the right to want this for themselves, they unconsciously sabotage their own efforts to support those they love and resent demands made on them. When an important relation does not allow for mutual dialogue, women feel disempowered.

The same applies to anger and power. Women's living as subordinate engenders anger that they feel they cannot express because they have been told that it is destructive to their sense of identity and because it threatens their lifework of enhancing relationships between people. Only men's anger is seen as legitimate. Similarly, women fear admitting that they want or need power since a woman's using self determined power for herself is usually seen as selfish and destructive, leading to attack and abandonment. A way out of this dilemma, it is suggested, is for women to be powerful in ways that simultaneously enhance, rather than diminish, the power of others. (Jordan et al. 1991, passim)

Although much has changed in the situation of women in the past years, the problematic tension between person and social role remains for them in a more aggravated form than for men. No one ever suggests that a career and fatherhood are incompatible, but, in the past at least, woman have often been told that they must choose between career and motherhood (with the obvious exception of single mothers who must work to support the family and women of color when the father is absent or un- or underemployed). Most of the responsibility in the family structure is placed upon the woman, and neither men nor society in general are willing to provide women with the structural means of handling both roles with any ease.

For some, a woman's choices are more restricted still: either she must marry and raise a family or face life with no identity at all.

This, too, is changing with the advent of short term commitments and "serial monogamy." But it still remains the case in many places. "There is also the fact," comments anthropological psychologist Dee Aker, former president of the University of Humanistic Studies, that women's choices are still restricted by historical, cultural mind sets advocated by the prevailing authoritarian and patriarchal regimes of fundamentalist religions. (For example, recent limited papal apologies for sexism notwithstanding, the Vatican documents for Beijing unrelentingly pushed what has come to be called "papal anthropology," a view of male and female nature in which men are normative persons and women are mothers.) The collective expectations of peoples' histories do not change easily, even if one generation departs from the given definition and tries to create new cultural norms. I think that is why backlashes such as the one we are in now take hold so easily. [Aker, 1998]

Basic to the cultural divisions of roles has been woman's reproductive role. The "pill" has modified this situation, but it has not fundamentally changed it. Society will not allow woman's reproductive role to be threatened; yet without freedom in this respect, all woman's other freedoms are in danger of being empty.

<u>The Fight for Equality and the Realm of the Between</u>

Another, equally essential, and corollary aspect of this battle for the empowerment of women is Buber's realm of the "between." Equality and dignity cannot be won by women themselves or by changing the attitude of any number of individual men. It must be won in the dynamic of lived and living relationship in the concrete situations in which men and women meet and confirm one another as man or woman *and* as person, holding the tension between these two so that, if they can never be simply identified, neither can they ever be separated. If modern man in general knows anxiety, alienation, and exile, it is certain that modern woman knows it in still fuller measure because she faces the simultaneous breakup of traditional values and of such traditional images of woman as might have satisfied her great grandmother, grandmother, or even her mother.

One cannot legislate the removal of sexual differences arising from the culture just by recognizing that they are the product of the culture and not merely of biological inheritance. The problem is no less real if it is borne by culture rather than by inheritance, though this may change our attitude toward it and give us some hope of changing it. All we can do, here as elsewhere, is to hold the tension between the person and the social role, recognizing the necessity of both and moving in the direction of greater freedom for every person to choose her own social role or roles and not have it imposed on them by others.

The Image of Woman and the Eclipse of the Human

The image of woman is not something that stands revealed once for all but a reality that is continually being revealed, or obscured, in each new situation. To say that the image of woman is in eclipse does not mean that we have no images of women: it means that the humanness of woman is left out of those images. It is precisely what woman as woman and as human being may, can, and ought to become that is often left out of both traditional and non traditional images of women.

Distancing May Lead to More Equal Relating

To stress, as we have, that the problem is one of the "between" and that the task is one that men and women must work on together is not to suggest that socially men and women are in an equal position of authority and power. Despite the gains that have been made in recent decades, women are still far down on the social scale. The greater power and responsibility still lies on the side of men in fighting the inequality of women.

Bias and the Women's Movement

If today's man in the modern world knows anxiety, alienation and exile, it is certain that his female counterpart knows it in still fuller measure. Faced with the simultaneous breakup of traditional values and their corresponding images of the woman in care giving, maternal, and subordinate roles, the Women's Movement has not been merely a rejection of traditional roles in the pursuit of more prestigious ones. It has been the struggle to make choices in a modern world that meet its demands without surrendering permanently to the anxiety, alienation, and exile that threaten to swallow them up. As much as women have struggled to effect legislative change to lay claim to a legitimate place in the modern world, legislation alone cannot remove the sexual biases arising from our culture.

As with equality, women's rights can only be achieved in the partnership of existence where differences between the sexes are not reduced to the point of men and women becoming androgens, but where men and women are validated both in social role and biological inheritance. Once again, the tension between person and social role must be held, recognizing the necessity of both and moving in the direction of the freedom of every person to choose their social role and not have it imposed on them by others.

The greatest problem in the struggle for gender equality might be in the steps and stages that must be gone through in order to reach a different, better relationship *between* the sexes. For women whose primary relationship is to other women there is also the need for dialogue and partnership. As women struggle to hold their ground in relationship to men, they may find comfort and support in pulling away at various points to strengthen their sisterhood with one another.

What will make this movement particularly meaningful in terms of the relationship between women and men will be the return to dialogue with men—not a more militant and defended return but one that leads to a stronger, more equal dialogue than before. The dialogue will evoke the human in men as well as affirm the human in women; thus strengthening the partnership of existence.[12]

In order for women to learn to hold their ground in relationship to men, therefore, they may have to pull away at various points and strengthen their sisterhood with one another. But this will be meaningful only if that distancing leads later to a stronger and more equal relating than before--in most cases in the relation of women to men but also in the relation of women to women. "This has been happening for the last five years or so," Dee Aker reported to me. "Women's search for equality, respect, and the recognition of human rights is no longer a white middleclass issue. Women are working across class and ethnic lines, and some men are joining them" (conversation, 1999).

When this takes place, the dialogue will evoke the human in men as well as affirm the human in women, and it will manifest the human image that lies hidden between the two. We need a new paradigm in which the competition between male and male, male and female, and female and female is steadily replaced by mutual respect. Hopefully, the "confirmation of otherness" that I have put forward for the last quarter of a century can help bring this new paradigm into existence.

PART THREE

PERSONAL UNIQUENESS, NON-VIOLENCE, AND RELIGIOUS PLURALISM

CHAPTER 11

Maintaining Personal Uniqueness in Community Institutions

The Life of Dialogue and Personal Uniqueness

Much has been said the last thirty years about the importance of realizing our human potentials. The "human potential movement" took root and flourished in the 60's and 70's. There are still many who follow the notions birthed during those years, namely, that we all contain great potential and that our highest human and moral obligation is to actualize it--by painting, writing, poetry, dancing, or whatever our gifts are. The life of dialogue does not think in terms of realizing "human potentialities". On the contrary, it is taken up with bearing witness to the unique person one is called to become. The unique person is not an individual who is different from other individuals but someone who becomes herself in relationship with others. She is unique because she is known only in and for herself. I know who you are because in the life of dialogue there is, first of all, you and me. I can bear witness to who you are in each lived moment and therefore know first-hand the uniqueness that makes you great in your own right.

Someone once spoke to the Hasidic rabbi Menahem Mendel of Kotzk comparing two acquaintances by name. When the Kotzker rebbe heard this, he exclaimed, "If I am I because I am I and you are you because you are you, then I *am* I and you *are* you. But if I am I because you are you and you are you because I am I, then I am not I and you are not you!" This is one of my favorite Hasidic Tales because it is an affirmation that we are each unique persons standing on our own ground and do not need to be better than someone else to have a sense of self-worth. In my book *Problematic Rebel,* I have characterized Dostoievsky's "Underground Man" as a consciousness plus a social role, precisely because he always felt superior or inferior to everyone he met but was not a person in himself. He is not unlike those of us in modern society who are pursuing our potentialities at the expense of our personal uniqueness.

The Hebrew Bible says that we have been created in the image of the imageless God, as a result of which each of us has a unique value and a unique created task that no other person has. This notion of "created uniqueness" was expanded and developed in Hasidism and was succinctly expressed by Rabbi Nachman of Bratzlav: "God never does the same thing twice." Martin Buber takes this idea a step further when he says, "Uniqueness is the essential good of man that is given him to unfold." Uniqueness is what makes a person of value beyond usefulness or function in relationship to others. To be a person is to be a center in itself called forth in the life of dialogue. Think of raising children.

Their uniqueness is not simply there nor is it imprinted on them. It is called out in response to teachers, classmates, the artistic task into which they have ventured, or the book that they are reading.

We all experience the imprint of our culture and of society, but our uniqueness shines in and through that imprint. An excellent example of this is supplied by Dr. Royal Alsup, a "liberation psychologist" who worked twenty years as a counselor for Native Americans. Royal Alsup wrote to me of the American Indian tribal way:

One belongs to a family tradition of hunting, boat makers, dance makers, artists, potters, dancers, or singers. But the individual stamp is on it because when somebody hears a dance song, they say that's Jimmy's song, or if they see a painting they say it's one by the Griffin brothers or Tripp's, or if they see a basket they say that's Nancy's. This experience of uniqueness is expressed in a family and tribal heritage. It is what separates meaning from no meaning for a person enveloped in a tribal culture.

It might appear that our uniqueness is identical with what is today called "self-realization." We need the freedom for self-development to be sure; yet, uniqueness, as we have seen, is not identical with the realization of our potentialities. Realizing our potentialities may be a meaningless endeavor if such realization is not anchored in the life of dialogue where our uniqueness is confirmed again and again in each lived moment. A man with many potentialities, Albert Schweitzer had to choose not only whether he would give the highest priority to being an organist, a theologian, or a missionary doctor in Africa, but also, and more significantly, between becoming one sort of person or another. The same holds true for you and me.

Our uniqueness is our personal vocation that is discovered when we are called out by life and become ourselves in responding. A tribal member, Royal Alsup points out, takes a risk when singing his or her new dance song in a ceremony. The confirmation by other tribal members telling him that was a great jump dance (a world renewal ceremony) or brush dance song (a healing ceremony for children) enables the tribal member to feel his own uniqueness —he feels that he is called to be a singer in the ceremonies.

We must respond to this call from where we are, and where we are is uniquely personal. Our very sense of ourselves comes only in our meeting with others as they confirm us in the life of dialogue. It is through this confirmation that we can grow to the strength of Socrates, who said, "I respect you, Athenians. But I will obey the god and not you." Socrates made his contribution when he expressed his responsibility to his fellow Athenians--precisely in opposing them. But if Socrates had not had seventy years of confirmation in the life of dialogue with his family of origin, his own wife and children, and the Athenians with whom he met in daily discussion, he would not have been able to stand his ground.

The uniqueness that one partner experiences in genuine dialogue with another is hidden from the individual who comes merely as objective observer, scientifically curious analyst, or prying manipulator. We cannot and will not allow another to "see into our soul" if we sense a prying, unsafe or indifferent presence. That is why a friend can know more about another friend's troubles than the trained psychologist with his Thematic Apperception tests even though the psychologist may provide a more accurate "objective" and clinical description of the friend's problem.

Once, when my wife Aleene was working in Scripps Clinic in San Diego, one of the two psychologists who were the titular heads of the Pain Clinic gave an assessment to a patient of Aleene's whom he had never met before. *"You* don't know me at all!" the patient exclaimed. "I know all I need to know about you," said the psychologist. "I have seen the results of your MMPI (Minnesota Multiphasic Personality Inventory)." If we sense that someone is trying to "psych" us out or find out what makes us tick, we shut off precisely those parts of us that make us unique persons regardless of our impulses toward investing our trust in experts.

Political Correctness

The catchword and slogan of the '90s was "political correctness." Some do not object to this because it encompasses more up-to-date views of sexual harassment, employer-employee relations, social customs, and political actions. By claiming to be politically correct, I feel, we are in danger of +no longer seeing ourselves as responsible for examining our lives, ourselves, and our actions toward others. To the extent that people endeavor to be politically correct at the expense of personal and social responsibility, the partnership of existence will suffer.

The partnership of existence espouses an approach to political, social, interpersonal, and family interactions that holds the tension between personal uniqueness and social role. This means that one's social role is informed and shaped by daily interactions with the world. A recent event in which a famous actor rescued a young person from being crushed by people crowding to get his autograph is a case in point. The actor was touted by the media as a hero and, as such, was the subject of public admiration. He was suddenly defined by a single action. The media searched its files on this individual to promote his heroism as something he was known for. By citing other incidents where the actor came to someone's rescue, he was being raised to a level of political correctness that might give others cause to overlook or disregard his unique response to a particular moment or circumstance.

The converse is also true. Individuals who are accused of being politically incorrect in today's world are characterized by the popular media and general public as villains, malcontents, non-conformists and crackpots. While this is not unique to our age or time, it has taken on a dimension and proportion that gives cause for concern. It's as though an impersonal, anonymous "they" has taken over the mastery of our social and personal lives.

Confirmation and Social Usefulness

All individuals stand not only in person-to-person and person-to-family relations but also, by the very nature of human society from the earliest times, in those technical relations that arise from the specialization of labor in which individuals serve social functions for other individuals. Against this Karl Marx complained when he said that workers are treated as commodities. As a result of this specialization of labor, a large part of the confirmation that is offered by one individual to another is in the nature of how each person functions in his or her social tasks and roles. There is nothing wrong with this. It is an absolute necessity of human existence. Yet from it arises the fact that our relationships not only include the confirmation of personal uniqueness but also the tendency to exploit and enjoy one another's individual abilities, usefulness, and charm. This primordial fact of human existence often leads to a standing mistrust, so that even when a person is being offered genuine personal confirmation, he or she is likely to ask, "Am I being offered this as myself?"

Franz Kafka caught the essence of this human dilemma in his story1 *The Metamorphosis.* Gregor Samsa is a traveling salesman. He spends his time during the day traveling to neighboring cities and selling a commodity the nature of which we are not told. In the evenings when he is free he has two forms of entertainment. One is to figure out train schedules for the early train he must take the next morning. The other is to do ornamental fretwork.

Gregor wakes up one morning to discover himself transformed into a gigantic insect. He shuts himself in his room. When his employer comes and reproaches him with being a bad son to his family and a bad worker, Gregor finally consents to open the door. The employer runs away in horror, and from then on Gregor lives more and more totally closed off in his room until finally the family no longer chooses to regard him as their son or brother. "It can't be my brother," his beloved sister says, "or he would not bother us," as he did when he came out once to hear her play the violin. He had been saving his money to send her to the conservatory and with the rest of it supporting his family since his father no longer worked. The father shows that he has resilience after all; he gets a job as a doorman with a splendid uniform replete with fine brass buttons. Gregor voluntarily starves to death with grateful thoughts of his parents while his family, rejoicing in his sister's blooming into young womanhood, goes off on a picnic.

Whatever else we might make of this tale, it is clear that Gregor had no true human existence even before his transformation. He was already shriveled up as a person, for he lived and was confirmed only in terms of his functions. When he is no longer in a position to be the breadwinner for his family or to send his sister to the conservatory, he loses all right to exist. The cleaning lady throws "the thing" out after Gregor has died, and the family is greatly relieved.

Though the metamorphosis was startling and sudden, it was no great transition for Gregor to go from being a cog in the economic machine to being an insect of no economic or social value. Charlie Chaplin's classic film, *Modern Times,* pictures a worker on an assembly line who is fed by a machine as he works, in order not to hold up production.

It is no accident that both these pieces of art stem from the twentieth century, for this absence of personal confirmation is particularly true of "modern times." The nature of our industrial and electronic society is such that one is hardly likely to get confirmed as a person in one's personal uniqueness. There is something about society as such that makes this threat of non-confirmation an integral part of the human condition. William Butler Yeats captured this in his beautiful poem, "For Anne Gregory":

> Never shall a young man,
> Thrown into despair
> By those great honey-coloured
> Ramparts at your ear,
> Love you for yourself alone
> And not your yellow hair.
>
> But I can get a hair-dye
> And set such colour there,
> Brown, or black, or carrot,
> That young men in despair
> *May* love me for myself alone
> And not my yellow hair.
>
> I heard an old religious man
> But yesternight declare
> That he had found a text to prove
> That only God, my dear,
> Could love you for yourself alone
> And not your yellow hair.

This does not mean that she can be loved *only* for her yellow hair, but it does mean that she cannot be loved apart from it or her eyes or her smile or her humor or charm.

Kyo, the hero of André Malraux's novel, *Man's Fate,* is told by his European doctor wife, May, that she has taken advantage of the freedom that they have agreed to give each other to sleep with a fellow doctor in the hospital who keeps pressing her to do so. Kyo's reaction is that she ought not to have used that freedom. To him it is a betrayal and one that is all the more painful coming as it does on the very brink of the Shanghai communist revolution of which he is the leader.

Nonetheless, at this very time, he thinks to himself that there are two sorts of people—those like his fellow Communist Party members who judge him by his actions and those like May who love him and who would love him even unto treason, suicide, or baseness of any sort. It is easy to understand why Kyo feels this way. Nonetheless, he is asking for something that no human being can ask for: to be loved as an essence that has nothing to do with his actions as a person.

Kyo has a right to ask that those who care about him not judge his actions simply from the outside. That is a different matter. He has a right to hope that those who love him try to understand the relation between himself and his action. He might even wish that they would remember what Kierkegaard said: "No person can judge another for no one knows how much of what he does is suffering and how much temptation," that is, in how much of his actions was he compelled to do what he did and in how much of them did he have some real freedom to do otherwise.[13] But he cannot go beyond that and claim that his whole person is some essence that is unconnected with his actions, his situation, and his relations to others.

There is no direct correlation between confirmation and being right or wrong. Some people have a history of being so unconfirmed that they can do the right thing again and again and still not take in the confirmation that may genuinely come their way. Other people are so self-confident that they can repeatedly do and say the wrong thing and still come off "smelling like roses."

It is common enough to find that the more money a person has, the greater is the authority with which he speaks about political and religious matters. But this is exactly what Socrates observed about the Athens of his time: all the poets knew about politics, and all the politicians knew about poetry. The reason that the oracle held Socrates to be the wisest man in Athens was that he was the only one who knew that he did not know! A large part of what appears to be confirmation is inextricably bound up with social status, one's place in the "pecking order," one's role in the family.

While it is true that people at the top of the pecking order feel misunderstood, unloved, depressed and isolated, the compassion we feel and energy we use to help "heal" them rarely finds its way to those at the bottom of the social order. Immigrants, homeless people, those with mental illness, inner-city poor, and even large numbers of suburban youth are held in contempt or disregarded. As a person's social status is increasingly defined by an impersonal culture and less by family, friends and mentors, politically correct responses to human dilemmas are less humane, more intolerant and increasingly "managed" by social systems that may or may not have any one person's best interests at heart.

The "Contract"

In addition to wholehearted personal confirmation, however, there is also what I call the "contract"—confirmation with strings attached. We will confirm you if you are a good boy or a good girl, or a good wife, or a good churchgoer,, a good citizen, or a good soldier. If we accept this contract—and most of us do—then we feel that it is not our selves that are being confirmed but only our acts that conform to other's expectations of us. This often splits us into an obedient part and a rebellious part. The need for confirmation is so great, in fact, that we often become what Martin Buber calls "seeming persons"—persons who put on a front or image that they imagine will win approval and confirmation from significant others.

In addition to wholehearted personal confirmation, however, there is also what I call the "contract"—confirmation with strings attached. We will confirm you if you are a good boy or a good girl, or a good wife, or a good churchgoer,, a good citizen, or a good soldier. If we accept this contract—and most of us do—then we feel that it is not our selves that are being confirmed but only our acts that conform to other's expectations of us. This often splits us into an obedient part and a rebellious part. The need for confirmation is so great, in fact, that we often become what Martin Buber calls "seeming persons"—persons who put on a front or image that they imagine will win approval and confirmation from significant others.

The paradox of needing to be confirmed and yet not being confirmed as ourselves originates in the family. But it becomes intensified and hardened as we move out into the social and economic roles that we must take upon ourselves to exist in human society. (Friedman 1983a, Chaps. 1-7)

Confirmation with strings attached is not necessarily bad. It's part of our social training, beginning with our family interactions, to be taught that obedience and cooperation are rewarded with recognition and praise. This conditional way of relating forms the contract that ultimately underlies our ways of being with others. The paradox of the "contract" becomes intensified and hardened as we move out into the social and economic roles that we must take upon ourselves to exist in human society. We realize our personal uniqueness when we answer the call that comes to us from the persons and situations in our lives. Each of us has need of the personal confirmation that can come only when we know we are answering to a call.

A young attorney struggling with depression and feelings of worthlessness could not find comfort in his six-figure job working for a nationally recognized law firm. This was the case even though he was following a path laid out by his family and many others that had groomed him for the position he now held. When asked what he really wanted to do with his life he replied, "I want to become a bush pilot in Alaska." The moment he announced what he really wanted to do he changed--as though breaking out of thick clouds into bright, blue skies.

He could not simply confirm himself. His obligation to fulfill his contract overrode his desire to pursue a direction that would meet with certain disapproval. We may be able to do without the admiration of crowds, but we cannot do without that silent dialogue through which we place our life-work within the context of our friendships and social responsibilities. We need to feel that our work is "true"-- both as a genuine expression of the reality that we encounter in our lives and as a genuine response to some situation or need that calls us.

Ronald Laing, who, like many psychologists and psychiatrists, was influenced by Buber's concept of confirmation, writes:

Every human being, whether child or adult, seems to require *significance,* that is, *place in another person's world.* Adults and children seek "position" in the eyes of others, a position that offers room to move. . . Most people at some time in their lives seek the experience, whether or not they have found it in early life, of occupying first place, if not the only significant place, in at least one other person's world. [14]

Laing, too, understands this universal human need for confirmation not only in terms of direct person-to-person relationships but also in terms of the complexities of group membership and social role:

Each group requires more or less radical internal transformation of the persons who comprise it. Consider the metamorphoses that one man may go through in one day as he moves from one mode of sociality to another—family man, speck of crowd dust, functionary in the organization, friend. These are not simply different roles: each is a whole past and present and future, offering differing options and constraints, different degrees of change or inertia, different kinds of closeness and distance, different sets of rights and obligations, different pledges and promises. I know of no theory of the individual that fully recognizes this.[15]

The Calling

Each of us must risk oneself to establish oneself as the person that one is and risk failure in so doing.[16] Paradoxically, this means that while the "calling" in its original meaning is an answer to a call, we have to take the first step ourselves and assert that we are called before the call comes. Each of us, no matter how thorough our training, experiences a moment of uneasy tension between our personal and professional selves when we first step forward as a "doctor," a "psychotherapist," a "minister," a "teacher," a "lawyer." or even a "husband," a "wife," a "father," or a "mother." At this moment the question, "What am I doing taking on this role?" may well produce an invisible inner panic that has nothing to do with competence or "self-confidence." This is the sense of incongruity that comes when one part of oneself is consciously "role-playing" while another part looks on and asks whether one can, in all good faith, identify oneself with this role. If we can make this venture "stick," then we shall be confirmed by others in our "calling" and soon will come to identify ourselves so much with our social role that our self-image will be unthinkable without it.

Another deeper problem is that of the tension between personal and social confirmation. The person who makes the assertion that he is a doctor or minister "stick" does not necessarily thereby receive personal confirmation. It may happen, on the contrary, that the more successful he is in his social role, the less he feels confirmed as a person. This is bound to be the case when a social role remains mere "role-playing" and is never integrated in any thoroughgoing fashion with one's personal self. This is particularly true of those whose social roles elevate them above the populace and make it necessary for them to pretend to attitudes, convictions, and ideals that they do not really hold.

Prince Charles' marriage to Diana Spencer was a modern example of this. He married her more for his subjects than for himself and the end result was a turbulent, then broken marriage. But it is also likely to be true of anyone who, in one's desperate need for the confirmation of others, prefers to sacrifice one's personal integrity rather than run the risk of not being established in a definite, socially-approved role.

Inequality is a burden for the caregiver in genuine community

Caring brings people together but not always as equals. This is particularly true in relationships between caring professionals and the people they serve. One person provides care for a recipient. The caregiver may view the recipient as the patient or client. The caregiver is presumed to be in better health than the patient who is being cared for. There is nothing new or significant in all this except when the very role of caring gets in the way of actual caring because the caregiver perceives the patient to be less human by virtue of his ailment or need. An author of a book on T-groups reported that the groups of nurses that he worked with tended to be less aware of the real needs and problems of their patients precisely because they saw them as "sick people." Perhaps this is why twenty-five hundred years ago, Lao-tzu joined being humble and being fair to caring as the three qualities he cherished:

When a man cares he is unafraid,
When he is fair he leaves enough for others,
When he is humble he can grow;
Whereas if, like men of today, he be bold without caring,
Self-indulgent without sharing,
Self-important without shame,
He is dead.
The invincible shield
Of caring
Is a weapon from the sky
Against being dead.[17]

The very existence of social roles means inequality of some sort, and the helping professions represent a built-in inequality of helper and helped in contrast to the unstructured and informal mutual give-and-take of some friends and some families. This inequality does not in itself prevent mutual respect and mutual trust as long as the attitude remains that of a person-to-person partnership. When the social role denotes some superiority of one person over another, this is no longer so, and when persons of whatever helping profession receive their own personal confirmation through feeling that *they* are the helpers and the others are the helped, the "patients," this mutuality is endangered.

In Kafka's story *The Metamorphosis* once Gregor Samsa is no longer able to speak, his family assumes that he cannot understand them and soon convince themselves that he is not really Gregor at all. This cruel story concerns the family, but how often is it also true of the terminally ill, the deaf, the mute, the blind, those who cannot speak or move due to a stroke, those who are transfigured by accident or disease so we do not recognize our own humanity in them? Whenever a nurse or doctor sees anyone first and foremost as a "patient," a member of the class of the sick, to be "helped" but not to be related to, there is the danger of that progressive decay of communication that may transform that person too, like Gregor Samsa, into a "thing."

Beyond Universalized Values

During my years of working closely with the Quakers I noted that they are fond of turning George Fox's answering "that of God in his enemies" into an affirmation of the goodness of humankind. I occasionally teased them by saying, "I love that of God in you. I just can't stand you!" What I meant, of course, is that such universal love is not love at all.

Rabbi Moshe Leib of Sasov said that he learned to love when he went to an inn where he witnessed the conversation of two drunken peasants. "Do you love me?" the first peasant asked the second. "I love you like a brother!" the second peasant answered. "*You* don't love me," rejoined the first peasant. "You don't know what I lack. You don't know what I need." The second peasant fell into a sullen silence. "But I understood," said Moshe Leib. "To love another is to understand his need and bear the burden of his sorrow." This is not human need in general. It is not even the need that one can deduce from the knowledge of a particular culture. It is the need of this real, other person in all her uniqueness, including all those things that shame or burden her.

Beyond Solicitude

To be in the world means to be together with others in the world -it means the "partnership of existence." Some see this relationship as one of solicitude. But solicitude cannot *as such* be an essential relation since it does not set a person's life in direct relation with the life of another, but only one person's solicitous help in relation with another person's lack and need of it. Even if one is moved with extreme pity, the barriers of one's own being are not thereby breached. One makes one's assistance, not one's self, accessible to the other. In real caring people participate directly in one another's lives, letting the mystery of the other enter into their own.

"Listening, not just hearing is central," says Patch Adams, the clown doctor made famous by the movie with his name. "When we gave up house calls, we gave up the gold." The doctor and patient "stand a better chance of making it through life's darkest moments as intimate and respecting partners, not in hierarchical roles." This means giving up the white coats and giving up the swooping down as a team on the "gall bladder" in the hospital bed. It also means giving up the quick, penetrating five-or-ten minute interview in favor of real dialogue, "learning about his or her parents, lovers, friendships, jobs and hobbies: the entire person."

Essential in all helping relationships is the mutuality of caring and concern. Even though the patient brings his or her problems to the therapist, the therapist still shares the concern about the sick family, the sick community, and the sick society that have generated those problems. Only through the person-to-person attitude of a partner can the therapist grasp the buried latent unity of the suffering person and of the social network from which that person comes.

A common situation, however, does not mean one that each enters from the same position or even a similar one. In caring relationships, the difference in position is not only that of personal stance, but also of role and function--a difference determined by the very difference of purpose that led each to enter the relationship. If the goal is a common one — the healing of the person — the relationship to that goal differs radically as between caregiver and the one who is cared for, and the healing that takes place depends as much upon the recognition of that difference as upon the mutuality of meeting and trust.

In helping relationships, moreover, inclusion is necessarily one-sided. The caregiver can neither demand nor expect that his client should experience his side of the relationship. Yet the one-sided inclusion of therapy is still an I-Thou relationship founded on mutual contact, mutual trust, and partnership in a common situation.[18]

The *paradox* of the caring relation is captured *par excellence* in the Hasidic story that I spoke pf above entitled "Climbing Down": "If you want to help another," one Hasidic rabbi said, "it is not enough to stand above and throw down a rope. Rather you must descend yourself into the mud and filth and then with strong arms pull yourself and the other up to the light." If you content yourself with standing above, you will not be able really to care for the other. On the other hand, if you go down into the "mud and filth," you risk being caught yourself in which case you will only succeed in dragging the other still further down. Really to care means to be able to enter into the situation of the other yet to bring with you some resources that the other does not have so that you may help make possible the healing that may come to pass in the *encounter* between you.

Caregivers often confess that they "become complacent" about patients' pain. One can only protect oneself from this overcaring by ceasing to make her pain present to oneself. Confronted with immediate pain, they are afraid of getting stuck in the mud and the filth. Confronted with their patients' fears of isolation and death, they remain above and throw down a badly frayed rope!

True Helping Means Balancing the Tension between Role and Response

But what else, you may ask, can you expect of a doctor or nurse who has to deal with a great many patients from all ways and walks of life? I do not expect any particular behavior from them, for I am well aware of the limitations of our understanding and resources. But our calling as helpers and caregivers asks us to hold the tension between our personal uniqueness and our caregiving roles so that we open the way for suffering persons to come to us.

To hold this tension means that we do not relegate ourselves as caregivers in person-to-person relationships to after work hours and weekends but move toward genuine dialogue in and through our social roles. Merely eliminating a social role does not bring persons into mutual relationship. Yet we need to be aware of the extent to which mutual mistrust is fostered in our present healthcare situation.

The Spirit of Openness, Risk, and Hope

If genuine community is to be real and effective, it must include a flexible, willing spirit able to withstand the concrete situation. Genuine dialogue means the recognition of real limits and real tragedy. But it also means hope because it does not assume that what was true this moment will necessarily be true the moment after -hope, not as idealism, therefore, but as a readiness to assess the new moment in its concreteness. This also means, of course, the readiness to know the needs of the other. Dialogue has to include the hope that will enable you to enter again, both actively and imaginatively, into the concrete situation of the other --tto risk and involve yourself and to discover in that situation what your resources are. We respond to what calls us with our actions and our lives —out of a concern as deep as the human, as real as the situation that faces us, as whole as we are able to be.

Such dialogue flowers into genuine community when our openness becomes a way of *interacting*. A psychiatric nurse who is the head of a community health project devoted to maternal and child-care hired a paraprofessional midwife of American Indian background to work in her project. "I am hopeful of learning more of the art of childbirth — all along the same path," the psychiatric nurse said. This is a step toward genuine community.

The Tension between Personal and Social Confirmation

The person who attempts to integrate his social role with his personal sense of direction and calling stands in the tension point between personal and social confirmation. One cannot resolve this tension by renouncing social confirmation, for no one can live without it. Everybody must play a social role, both for the sake of economic livelihood and as the simplest prerequisite for any sort of relations with other people in the family and society. On the other hand, one cannot resolve the tension by sacrificing personal confirmation, for this suppression of a basic human need results in an anxiety that may be more and more difficult to handle as the gap between person and role widens.

To keep our social role in tension with personal uniqueness is not easily done. Women are particularly in tune with this struggle as they seek to balance the demands of their professional lives with those of their personal lives as partners, mothers and friends. Men too are aware of the fight and often complain that there is no role, at work or home, in which they feel a sense of personal uniqueness.

We cannot deny the specialization of labor and the continual rationalization of that specialization that creates the need to call for people as abstractions, such as professor, secretary, machinist, crane operator, doctor, or bank clerk. But job descriptions, while important, do not necessarily define our true abilities, talents or interests. Our social roles are not entitled to so exhaust our resources and reserves that we have nothing left to give to our personal existence. The unique relationship we have to our work is important not just for the work's sake but for the meaning we seek for our own lives as individuals who must exist with more than a thread of authenticity.

To the extent that we recognize the necessity for a continual critique of the categorical abstractions around which we must relate, we can reject the unfair "burden of always responding to a situation in a catalogued way." This means to reject a life in which we are all but smothered under the weight of technical, social, and bureaucratic abstractions. This is a cultural and spiritual revolution that must concern us all. It is my belief that this resistance to the impersonal is at the root of much of the modern rebellion we see and hear – especially from the segments of our society that are lowest in the pecking order.

In many spheres we come upon the plain signs of the fragility of our life together, of the life between person and person. Our hope for the "greening" of America or the world can be meaningful only if we begin with the realism that shows us caught in an immense corporate state or network of military and industrial complexes. The pervasive alienation that results disables our ability to be with one another in community. The realization of our personal uniqueness that can only come in that being together is replaced with pseudo-freedoms that we imagine we enjoy. But if there is a fragility in our life as human beings there is also strength. The deeper the human image is hidden, the greater the possibility that resources may arise from the depths through which we can rediscover in each situation the human being, man, woman and child.

CHAPTER 12

Genuine Community, Non-Violence, and The Covenant of Peace

Social Action and the Partnership of Existence

We must have social planning and social action, but communities should not approach social action like a game of chess where strategies to gain power are set forth. Genuine community calls for social action that arises out of true dialogue. Unfortunately, our whole notion of social action—that we use *this* means to *that* end—plainly ignores the fact that we do not know what the consequences are going to be of almost any action that we perform.

A director of one particular social action group said, "If we don't stop abortion, who will defend the rights of unborn children?" Those in support of his cause may agree that abortion must be stopped. Some would even suggest that any means, even violent means, would be justified. The rationale is that abortion is evil and must be met with forceful resistance. To them, violence, as a means to an end, is an acceptable social action. But is violence an option for genuine community? Does any community have the right to use social action with such force as to eliminate a perceived threat? These and more difficult questions challenge us as we move into the new millennium.

How can we know what the impact of our social action will be in advance? Does the anti-war protester know that his hunger strike will end the war? Did Martin Luther King know that his efforts to help blacks achieve social equality in the United States would take generations to realize? We make the mistake of thinking that we know the impact our social action will have because it happens *through* us. Yet we do not even know our own resources, much less the situation that will confront us. We can plan the *structure* within which social action will take place, but we should refrain from planning the events themselves until we have discovered what our response should be. Such discovery requires us to flounder between action and indecision. We must struggle and search for ways to stand our ground in the face of social ills that threaten to undo us and taunt us to fight.

Conflict and Reconciliation

Each of us must do our share to build true community. Reality is not given in me alone or in some part of reality with which I identify myself. Even in genuine community, there is no single, unifying vision that will merge my reality with yours so as to eliminate potential conflict. This introduces a tension whereby we may regard those unlike ourselves as less than human in some way. Among primitive tribes, the members of other tribes were often not even considered human beings. Even the civilized Greeks saw the rest of the non-Greek world as "barbarians" and therefore by nature unequal to them and properly forced into permanent slavery when conquered. On the coast of Africa there are still great castles in which for four hundred years the Portuguese, the Dutch, and the English vied with one another as to who would get the most profit from shipping fifty million slaves to America for sale there.

The ravaging of the American frontier and the ravages of the whaling industry, similarly, show that a good deal of what has characterized modem man, long before the Nazi exterminations, has been a lack of respect for the otherness of creation, including

125

the non-human part of it. Since the Nazis this relation to nature has continued with a whole series of ecological disasters that grow ever-more threatening year by year: oil spills, water-use abuse, deforestation, pollution, failure to dispose properly of toxic wastes or to recycle non-biodegradable products.

The respect for the otherness of the other does not mean that I love everyone or even that I have the resources to meet everyone in genuine dialogue. But it does mean that everything that confronts me demands my attention and response — whether of love or hate, agreement or opposition, confirmation or merely letting be.

The greatest task confronting us is not to build "enlightened" utopias but to build peace in the context in which we find ourselves. The true peacemakers are those who take upon themselves, in the most concrete manner conceivable, the task of discovering what can be done in each situation of tension and struggle by way of facing the real conflicts and working toward genuine reconciliation.

"A peace without truth is a false peace," said Rabbi Mendel of Kotzk. What "truth" means here is made clear by the Talmudic statement the Hasidic master partly quoted: controversies for the sake of heaven endure. We cannot build true peace by ignoring conflict. In controversies each is a witness to her own "touchstone of reality." Recognizing this enables us to confirm the other in her truth even while opposing her. We do not have to liberate the world from those who have different witnesses from us. We cannot confirm ethnic cleansing, but we have no right to obliterate even those whose life stance we must morally oppose.

This imaginative task of comprehending a relationship from the other side as well as ones own is essential to the goal of overcoming war, for every war justifies itself by turning the enemy into a Manichaean figure of pure evil, as Reagan did by calling the Soviet Union the "evil empire" and the elder Bush did by comparing Saddam Hussein to Hitler and Bill Clinton by comparing Slobedon Melosovich to the same.

Social Reality and Political Abstraction

The mistrust between nations makes them deal with each other not in social or human terms but in terms of political abstractions and catchwords. We cannot afford to be purely political, purely external. We must build on social reality and find its roots in the community already there. We must be concerned about real communication with the people whom we approach.

The distinction between propaganda and education does not lie in whether we are Communists or pacifists but in whether we approach another wishing to impose our truth on him or her or whether we care enough for the other to communicate our truth within the dialogue we share. Sometimes that dialogue can only mean standing our ground as opponents to the other, witnessing for what we believe in the face of their hostile rejection. Yet, even as opponents we must remain concerned for how the other sees reality. A reality opposing ours is not necessarily in "error." We must confirm our opponents in their existence as human beings whom we value even when we oppose them.

A genuine climate of trust elicits the "other voice," the voice of the person who will speak only in an atmosphere that weighs every voice equally no matter how hesitant or how much in the minority it may be. From 1921 until his death in 1965 Martin Buber continued to insist that Jews live *with* the Arabs in Palestine and later Israel and not just *next* to them and to warn that the way must be like the goal—*Zion bmishpat* ("Zion with justice")—that the humanity of our existence begins where we become responsible to the situation by saying: "We shall do no more injustice than we must to live, " and by drawing the "demarcation line" each hour anew in fear and trembling. The covenant of peace --between person and person, between community and community, and between nation and nation — means keeping an open path to dialogue.

Bringing Conflict into Dialogue

Dialogue means the meeting with the other person, the other group, the other people --a meeting that confirms the other yet does not deny ourselves and the ground on which we stand. The choice is not *between* ourselves and the other, nor is there some objective ground to which we can rise above the opposing sides, the conflicting claims. Rather genuine dialogue is at once a confirmation of community *and* of otherness, and the acceptance of the fact that we cannot rise above the opposing sides.

During three years of work in the 1950s as chairman of the American Friends of Ihud (the Israeli association for Israel-Arab rapprochement led by Judah Magnes and Martin Buber), I was again and again surprised to encounter among persons of good will, including persons working for reconciliation of the conflict, either an attitude that simply did not take into account the real problems to be reconciled, one that saw these problems from one point of view only, or one that proceeded from some pseudo-objective, quasi-universal point of view above the conflict.

Every conflict has at least two sides. Even if one of the two sides is "dead wrong" in its opinion or stand, it represents something real that cannot be done away with. The different point of view of each person must be recognized quite apart from the question of the rightness or wrongness of the position taken.

All too often, the word "reconciliation" becomes associated with a sentimental good will that looks away from the very conflict that is to be reconciled or assumes that with this or that action or approach a tragic situation can be transformed into a harmonious one. Genuine reconciliation must begin with a fully realistic and fully honest recognition of real differences and points of conflict. It must move from this recognition to the task of discovering the standpoint from which some real meeting may take place, a meeting that will include *both* of the conflicting points of view and will seek new and creative ways of reconciling them.

In the past in the Middle East every Arab voice calling for moderation was systematically silenced by those who want to keep the situation polarized, and the government in Israel has often seemed to settle into a position of permanent intransigence. Nonetheless, how can we doubt that there is a direction in which we must move with such resources as we can find, *quantum satis,* drawing the demarcation line anew in every hour?

The Covenant of Peace

The covenant of peace is neither technique nor formula and still less is it a universal principle that needs only be applied by deduction to the particular situation. It takes its start from the concrete situation, including all of its tensions --tensions that we can never hope or even desire to remove entirely since they belong to the very heart of genuine community.

The covenant of peace is no ideal that one holds above the situation, but a patient and never finished working toward some points of mutual contact, mutual understanding, and mutual trust. It builds community by way of the mutual confirmation of otherness, and when this community shipwrecks, as it again and again tends to do, it takes up the task anew. The covenant of peace means a movement *in the direction of* genuine community, such movement as each new hour allows.

Genuine community grows out of conflict within mutual cooperation, mutual understanding, and ultimately mutual trust. But in bedrock situations even a negative protest may be a positive step toward dialogue if it is done in the spirit of dialogue. The covenant of peace implies a "fellowship of reconciliation" yet it is precisely here that we have fallen short. We have tended to turn "reconciliation" into a platform to expound, a program to put over, and have not recognized the cruel opposition and the real otherness that underlie conflict.

We have been loath to admit that there are tragic conflicts in which no way toward reconciliation is at present possible. We have been insufficiently tough-minded in our attitude toward love, turning it into an abstract love for mankind or a feeling within ourselves rather than a meeting between us and others. We cannot really love unless we first know the other, and we cannot know her until we have entered into relationship with her.

A Listening Witness

Only a real listening --a listening witness --can plumb the abyss of that universal existential mistrust that stands in the way of genuine dialogue and peace. The Peace Movement has not adequately recognized the power of violence in our day nor that its roots are not just in human nature in general or in the stupidity of individuals but in the special malaise that we experience --our lack of a meaningful personal and social direction; our lack of an image of the human; our loss of community; our basic loss of trust in ourselves and others and in the world in which we live; our fear of real confrontation with otherness; our tendency to cling to the shores of institutionalized injustice and discrimination. Rarely do we see individuals or communities that are willing to set out upon the open seas of creating new and more meaningful structures within which the "wretched of the earth," the dispossessed and the systematically ignored, can find their voice too. The true heart of the covenant of peace is genuine community.

Violence and Non-Violence

In the absence of genuine community, in our day the dispossessed and the systematically ignored have found their voice through terrorism. This raises the question of the relation of genuine community to violence and nonviolence.

Although in general nonviolence confirms otherness and violence disconfirms it, nonviolence may disconfirm otherness when it is used as a tool of monologue and, in a limited sense at least, violence may confirm it. Nonviolence may be, and sometimes is, covert violence, congealed violence, suppressed violence, apocalyptic rage, perfectionist intolerance. It was not these things in Gandhi, A.J. Muste, and Martin Luther King; for in them it was grounded in personal existence and in genuine relationship to other persons, rather than objectified into an omnicompetent technique.

If we make the distinction that should be made between the force that sets necessary limits and the violence that destroys its object, we shall not imagine that violence ever confirms the otherness and uniqueness of the persons on whom it is used. But we can, in an age of terrorism, recognize the paradoxical fact that occasionally the terrorist's acts of violence, like the acting out of the child within the family system, are an attempt to call attention to the otherness of a minority group or people that has been ignored and passed over in the "general harmony," the violence of the status quo.

As Ivan Illich has pointed out, the worldwide growth of two societies, separate and unequal, should make clear the dynamics that provoke violence between them. The one society is the immensely rich economy of the United States; the other is the capital-starved economies of Latin America, the Third World, and the black ghettos.

Today the newly-independent countries of the former Soviet Union and the conflicting ethnic and national groups in what was Yugoslavia add to economic violence that of national, ethnic parochialism. Nor should we leave out of account differing standards of living, the resurgent anti-Semitism and growing racism in England and Western Europe, and Tienaman Square in the People's Republic of China. All these complicate the incidence of violence worldwide, even while the ending of the "cold war" offers hope of relief in the piling up of nuclear weapons.

Violence is the product of frustration, rage, shame, envy, the product of all those things that Rainer Maria Rilke called "unlived life." Unlived life itself is something more than the failure to express yourself or to dominate others, though that is what the romantic often thinks. It is the failure to give our passions direction by bringing them into the dialogue with the other human beings with whom we live --in our family, in the community, in the neighborhood, in the city, and in the country.

The failure to give our passions direction has to do with the fact that we do not take our stand, that we do not make our objection when we must, that we allow a pseudo-harmony to continue to exist. Often we cannot do otherwise, for we do not even consciously know that we have another point of view than that of the dominant group. Or if we do know it, we know the consequences of not staying "in our place." This goes right through our society --not just among the poor and underprivileged, but in the worlds of business, commerce, and government.

Violence is often the response, provoked by the sense of powerlessness and apathy, to a situation that is felt to block off all other ways of response. Violence also arises from mutual mistrust, including the mistrust of language. When the bond between human beings is destroyed and the possibilities for communication break down, aggression and violence occur.

Simone Weil defined violence as reducing a person to a thing the ultimate of which is killing, i.e., reducing a person to a corpse. If that is so, then violence can no more be avoided in our culture or any culture than we can avoid the "I-It relation," that is, the relation in which we use and know, classify and categorize one another, for this is an enormous part of our culture and becomes more so every day. It is these very categories, indeed, that lead us in the first place to prejudice, racism, and violence.

But if violence means converting the human Thou into an It, then violence is no more always inevitable than the domination of the It. We live in an age, God knows, in which the electonic machine, the corporation, and the technocrat dominate to an incredible degree. Yet a real possibility remains, through fighting and standing our ground, of bringing these back into human dialogue. It remains with us and cannot be removed by the fist of any number of economic, psychological, social, military, or political realists who say, "This is the way it is." But if we are going to take this possibility seriously, then in each concrete situation we have to discover the hard way what the resources are for dialogue and for creating something human, to bring the passion that explodes into violence into a real interchange.

Genuine Community and the Covenant of Peace

What we need for our time is an openness, a flexibility, a willingness to resist and withstand the concrete situation. This also means, of course, the readiness to know the needs of the other. A failure to recognize his or her needs is what the African American properly accuses the white person of. How can you say you are for brotherhood, peace, integration, progress, when you don't even hear me, when you don't imagine concretely what it means to live in the ghetto, to be black?

Dialogue, therefore, has to include not just hope of something happening but hope that will enable us to enter again, both actively and imaginatively, into the concrete situation of the other--to witness, to risk ourselves. to involve ourselves, to stand there and discover in that situation what the resources are.

Concrete Social Reality vs. Political Catchwords

We have been deluded by the notion that political power is the only power. Of course, political power is great power, and usually behind it are economic power and military power. Yet a large part of what we call politics is only the facade --a facade of catchwords, slogans, pretenses, nuances, innuendo, and downright lies. In fact, reality is more basically social, even though the political always tries to get more power and domination than it needs. In 1954 the Supreme Court struck down the "separate but equal" clause of the Interstate Commerce Act. We have learned to our great cost that this decision was necessary but not sufficient, that it has to become a social reality in every neighborhood, and it is not just law enforcement alone that is going to do that.

Concrete reality is found first of all in actual social living. This reality of our actual human and social life takes a while to manifest itself. But it is there beneath the surface, awaiting the day when social suffering will transform itself into unmistakable social movement. If we lose sight of the concrete and everything becomes tactics, then we also lose sight of the actual goal toward which we are working.

Gandhi's *Satyagraha*

This recognition of the human factor in the confrontations of our age can lead us to a new and deepened appreciation of Gandhi's *satyagraha*. This "soul-force," or "truth-force," should not be understood as a universal metaphysical, political, or ethical theory but as an image of the relations between person and person and between person and society.

Gandhi was very clear in his teachings that *satyagraha* is not a technique to be applied in miscellaneous acts but a way of life that has to arise out of the deepest human attitudes. "A little true non-violence acts in a silent, subtle, unseen way and leavens the whole society." But this nonviolence is not a method that can be taught, like judo or karate. It is the quality of the life that takes place between person and person.

Gandhi's *satyagraha* cannot be applied to all situations regardless of who is applying it. It is a direction of movement within the interhuman, the social, and the political that brings persons away from the vicious circles of violence and toward cooperation and mutual respect. Only insofar as *satyagraha* is permeated by the life of dialogue and concretely embodied in the meeting between person and person will it be able to fulfill the claims that Gandhi made for it.

Martin Luther King, Non-Violence, and Community

Martin Luther King was close in spirit to both Gandhi and Buber in his fight for true community and his confirmation of otherness through non-violence. Non-violence "does not seek to defeat or humiliate the opponent, but to win his friendship and understanding." Its goal is the "creation of the beloved community." *Agape,* to King, "is love seeking to preserve and create community. It is insistence on community even when one seeks to break it." There can be no split here between love and the demands of justice. Non-violent resistance, to King, is the narrow ridge between acquiescence and violence. King saw segregation in Buber's terms as substituting an "I-It" relation for an "I-Thou" relationship and relegating persons to the status of things. To stand, as King did, for the I-Thou relationship is to stand for the other as well as oneself It is to stand, in King's own language, for the dialogue between person and person eventually enlarging the concept of brotherhood to a vision of total interrelatedness.

Recognizing that power is not evil in itself but is the ability to achieve purpose, King deplored the common tendency to contrast the concepts of love and justice as polar opposites so that love becomes the resignation of power, power the denial of love. The major crisis of our time is this collision of immoral power with powerless morality.

Non-Violence in the Present

Happily, non-violence is not dead in the present world. On the contrary, all over the globe there are people who are carrying forward what Thoreau, Tolstoy, Gandhi, A. J. Muste, and Martin Luther King began. One of the most notable of such leaders is Mubarak Awad, Palestinian advocate for non-violence. Awad acknowledges the role that numerous women leaders in Palestine have played in his movement because these women, in contrast to men, do not want to see any more killing and death. Influenced by Gandhi's Muslim followers, Awad founded the Palestinian Center for the Study of Non Violence in Jerusalem in the early 1980s. He has also recorded the stories of older Palestinians who participated in non-violent activities, thus being able to offer his fellow Palestinians a native image to be followed rather than having to point to Gandhi and Martin Luther King.

Genuine Dialogue and Nuclear Disarmament

We cannot conclude this chapter without speaking of the ultimate violence that hangs heavily over our heads. Listening to a mass rally against nuclear armament sponsored by Physicians for Social Responsibility I was struck once again by the conviction that the *only* alternative to these preparations for the unwilled but technically perfect suicide of mankind is precisely that genuine dialogue for which Martin Buber called forty and fifty years ago. Only such dialogue contains the possibility of the confirmation of otherness that is not based on any sentimental overlooking of conflict but upon the readiness humanly to arbitrate the conflict through each of the partners, even when it stands in opposition to the other, heeding, affirming, and confirming its opponent as an existing other.

CHAPTER 13

Interreligious Dialogue and Touchstones of Reality

For many years now, we have been beset by a political polarization and an either/or mentality that has led us to shun complexity in favor of simple black versus white choices. Slogans, sound-bites and pseudo-solutions have been substituted for considered decisions. I am, in consequence, devoting this last part of the book to setting my own concept of the "dialogue of touchstones" in tension with the current cultural trends that value form over substance.

Touchstones of Reality

There is no reality independent of what I call touchstones of reality and no touchstone independent of contact with another in genuine dialogue. Touchstones of reality only come when we have fought our way through to where we are open to something really other than our accustomed set of values and our accustomed ways of looking at the world. I came to my touchstones not through the values that I already had but through the conflict between those values --a conflict that was only resolved by reaching continually new positions and with them new or transformed values. Outside the stream of living where each new situation renews my touchstones in a way that permits me to grow and change, I run the risk of my touchstones becoming a stagnant collection of insights that are hollow by comparison.

Touchstones and Communication

We live in a world where communication is taught as a management technique. A supervisor may say, "I hear you" in response to a complaint when she heard nothing you said at all. Once again, the touchstone of genuine meeting has been commuted to a communication technique where people are invited to share feelings that may later be used against them. A form of genuine meeting is being "taught" as a technique that--- by virtue of its lack of genuine interest on the part of one or more participants --breeds a climate of mistrust. One woman said, "I'm afraid to tell my supervisor how I really feel about her leadership. She'll take it out on me at review time."

People today think that by agreeing on abstractly defined terms such as equal opportunity or non-discrimination, we relieve ourselves of the need to "communicate" our touchstones of reality. People presume to understand one another if they agree on certain "important" terms that may be little more than catch phrases or buzz-words. One motto in an educational setting for children boasts that, "each child is a person of great worth." Who can disagree with that? By believing in this motto, however, can we assume that we know what each child needs?

Communication as a dialogue of touchstones means surrendering *both* the objective, universalist approach to the truth and the subjective emotional approach. We are alone with our touchstones, but if they are real, the one thing that someone else is sure to meet in any genuine meeting is our touchstones, not our insights and platitudes. More than leaving us with a general impression of another person's problem or situation, touchstones of reality bear witness to our having shared in another person's suffering or joy even after the situation has passed and the person has gone. The partnership of existence is the life-stream where we prove, probe, test and authenticate our touchstones.

Touchstones as Witnesses to our Lives

When two people really touch each other as persons --whether physically or not --the touching is not merely a one-sided impact: it is a mutual revelation of life-stances. Our touchstones are witnesses, as when Rabbi Leib said he came to the Maggid of Mezritch not to hear him say Torah but to watch the way in which he laced and unlaced his felt boots!. If we cherish our touchstones in our inwardness as sacred altars and do not witness for them with our lives, they atrophy and become sentimental ideals.

Many of us find our touchstones in partnership with others, the shared sense of reality of a football team that works well together, the fellowship of friends or even, occasionally, a fraternity or sorority, or the common struggle for a cause that we have made our own. What is more, some of us find our touchstones of reality through our unique response to the touchstones of others as they are communicated to us in a novel, play, or poem, an act of friendship or love, or just the way in which someone lives his or her life.

Even if I empathize or identify with your experience in a powerful way, the experience itself belongs to you and can never be mine. For this reason, touchstones do not bring us together in a merging of identities or ideals-- they define the lines between us and our experiences, making it possible for each of us to stand for ourselves while we bear witness to one another's lives. When we really witness, we do not abstract what we have to say from the event in which it took root.

We cannot hand the event over as an objective fact minus the interpretation that we have made of it. For this reason we have the right to ask those to whom we witness not to limit themselves to the words that we use minus the person using them and what we are witnessing to in our own life.

If communicating a touchstone means witnessing, then that witness can never be made with words alone. It must always include gestures, actions, pregnant silences, and the reality of the present moment itself. We cannot share something really unique with unique persons in a unique situation by abstracting from that uniqueness and looking only at the words that are used. Scientists may build a conceptual common reality through such abstractions, but as persons we must share the whole of our touchstones. When we bring what is uniquely our own into a common reality the possibility for sharing life-stances and, at times, friendship or community unfolds.

How Touchstones Are Communicated in Genuine Dialogue

Since touchstones are born out of an exchange in which two people genuinely touch, they can only be communicated in genuine dialogue. So much of the dialogue that exists between people today is, on one extreme, too combative, self-serving and suspicious to the point of paranoia to open the way for genuine meeting. On the other extreme, people are careful to the point of being passive in the interest of maintaining a civility that offends no one---what we call today "political correctness". We can only really touch if we are willing both to be open and to respond personally. We must also open ourselves to the possibility that the outcome of our time together may be different than either of us expects or plans.

Listening and Opposing

We have no right to judge the touchstones of others. If I morally condemn you, then I am excluding your reality with your touchstones. I am saying, in effect, "You have no right to make a witness." I have already defined your witness out of existence before it is made. But there is an "evaluation" that I cannot rightfully escape: I must hear you and I must respond. You need to know that you are really coming up against me as a person with touchstones and witnesses of my own.

Sometimes the strongest opposition is by far more confirming than someone who defends your right to your opinion under the general umbrella of "everyone has the right to an opinion" but does not take it seriously. Once at a Friends (Quaker) weekend on "Religion and Psychology" that I led at Haverford College a member of the faculty panel recognized ruefully that she had failed to respond meaningfully to another member of our Working Party for the future of the Quaker movement, to whifh I also belonged.. He asked her in particular to read the manuscript of his book on mysticism. After she read it, the only comment that she made was that she saw what he meant. She did not share her own personal views, including her criticisms and opposition. The real "dialogue of touchstones" means that we respond from where we are *and* that we bring *our* touchstones into the dialogue.

Sharing Our Touchstones

Although we each have our own viewpoint, we are not completely alone. We help one another along the road when we share our touchstones and the confusion that sometimes accompanies them. We evolve our touchstones in relationship with one another; we witness to one another. We have an impact on one another that causes us to grow in our own touchstones. Growing in this way, we come to recognize how touchstones of reality and the dialogue of touchstones, more than any creed or sacred tradition, keep the partnership of existence relevant and alive.

Fundamentalism World Wide

Not only in America but all over the world there has been a strong upsurge of what is called "fundamentalism" and with it the attempt to avoid the complexities that come from more thoughtful points of view. Many people world over have found both security and faith through accepting fundamentals of religion and the way of life that goes with it. This is by no means simply a Christian phenomenon, for there are very strong Islamic counterparts of Christian fundamentalism, and the same is true of some of the other religions, not excluding Judaism.

I do not need to elaborate here on this phenomenon, for it is too well known to require further description. What I wish rather is to set up against it my own claim that the only realistic position for us contemporary human beings is religious pluralism.

Moving toward a Spirit of Understanding

Every voice needs to be heard precisely because it represents a unique relationship to reality. Even though that voice may be distorted, "sick," and miserable, it still contains the nucleus of a unique touchstone that its very negativity both bears and conceals. People in our culture, especially the educated and the refined, fear being put down because the emphasis in today's society is on the quick and facile response.

The "community of affinity" protects itself through the either/or. Either you are one of us or you are not. If you are one of us, we do not need to hear you because we already know and represent your point of view. If you are different and if you disagree, we do not want to hear you because you "make waves" --you disturb the harmony of our like-mindedness.

Our society itself is sick -- polarized into communities of affinity. Because this is so, individuals cannot help being sick, since they do not have the ground on which to stand and from which to enter into the partnership of existence bringing with them their own touchstones of reality.

The third alternative to the sickness of conformity and the sickness of rebellion is the community that confirms otherness. Such a community gives each person a ground of her own, a ground in which mutual confirming and healing through meeting can take place in spiraling circles that bring more and more of each person's touchstones into the reality of life together.

The Dialogue of Touchstones as an Alternative to Absolutism vs. Relativism

The appeal to unanimity and universality is a thing of the past. Relativism, on the other hand, is the sickness of universalism turned inside out. It does not accept things as they happen in their uniqueness, for it knows only difference--comparison and contrast in terms of categories. In contrast to the either/or of absolutism and relativism, I offer as a genuine and more fruitful third alternative the mutual confirmation of the dialogue of touchstones.

This third alternative is difficult at first to grasp, for many people feel that we have to choose between an exclusivist truth, such as the fundamentalists who insist that theirs is the only true religion, and a hopeless relativism, such as those who reduce religion to the social construct of one culture or another. In contrast to both positions, I feel that *the reality of pluralism must be the starting point of any serious modern faith*.

We should give up looking for the one true religion founded on "Truth" and consider our religious commitments, through our unique relationships to it, to a truth to which we cannot lay claim. The "absolute" is still present here but not as a universal. We meet one another within the bond between the absolute and the "lived concrete."Any religious group based on commonly ascribed-to catch phrases or belonging for the sake of belonging is a pseudo-community. In contrast, the community that confirms otherness brings people together in a fellowship to which they relate from unique perspectives and life-stances.

The True Fellowship of the Committed

The true fellowship of the committed is that of persons who can meet and talk with one another because they really care about one another and the common goal they are serving, however differently that goal may be stated. This fellowship is often found not within but across organizational, institutional, and denominational lines. It is my experience that I can talk to a committed person of any religion or even no religion at all better than I can talk to an uncommitted person of my own religion. But this is not the case when religious commitment falls into the idolatry of objectifying one's touchstones of reality into universal truths and the wish to impose these truths upon others.

If this is so, then the answer to the dilemma of cultural relativism is not a new universalism or a new absolutism, nor even some "perennial philosophy" that claims to have found the true essence of all religions, but a religious pluralism--a mutually confirming dialogue of touchstones.

Accepting Religious Pluralism

"The solution to the problem of religious pluralism is not to collapse or do away with individual religious traditions," writes Harold Coward, "but rather to affirm and respect the faith of others."[19] We do not need to use the same words as others or even to affirm that beneath our different words and images we really mean the same thing in order to share a meaningful religious fellowship. We can accept the fact that we not only have different paths but also that these different paths may lead to different goals. What matters is that in listening to the other we hear something genuine to which we can respond. Real religious fellowship does not begin with creed or catechism but with genuine trust. As I have written in my book *A Heart of Wisdom*,

The structures of religion--creed, cult, and church--more often further a community of affinity, or like-mindedness, than they do a community of otherness. What is more, by their very claim to have a corner on the spirit and by their tendency to regard religion as the refuge from the mundane world, religious institutions and groups more often intensify the dualism between spirit and the world than overcome it.[20]

Lived Community of Trust as the Ground of Faith and Creed

Some religions, to be sure, seek to articulate abstract criteria of faith and creed. But unless those abstractions are rooted in lived tradition and lived community of trust, they are worthless. On the other hand, even the silence of a gathered Quaker meeting, which dispenses with all concepts, should not deceive its members into thinking they have attained unity during the meeting. The most we can responsibly speak of is community and communion, which enable the members of a fellowship to be fundamentally different yet really together.

Pseudo-Interreligious Dialogue

There has thrived in our day a form of pseudo-dialogue in which official representatives of religions carry on official dialogues that are neither genuine meetings of religions, for religions cannot meet, nor genuine meetings of persons because these persons speak only for their social role and do not stand behind what they say with their own persons. On the other hand, there is a new spirit of openness abroad among many religious thinkers. Real listening is already a form of responding, and real response is not only dialogue but also sharing from a different side in a common reality.

True Community as the Goal of the Dialogue of Touchstones

We cannot have the notion of "one truth" of which our individual religious truths are so many symbolic expressions. Every one of us has to witness from where he or she is. We shall never find a common philosophy, theology, or myth that in the end unites us. But we can share our myths with one another.

The ultimate issue and goal of the dialogue of touchstones is not communication but community -- lived togetherness of really unique persons, families, and groups. This is no formula. We should not claim to accept someone if that acceptance is conditional upon his or her reflecting the dominant coloration of the group.

²¹The Mutually Confirming Dialogue of Touchstones

The only "perennial philosophy" that I can and do espouse is that of openness--the witness to the ever-growing dialogue with committed persons of every religion and none. Each of the religions and each of the touchstones that I have entered into dialogue with have pointed me toward greater openness, and each has opened for others on the way the possibility of a fuller and freer fellowship--a mutually confirming dialogue of touchstones.

I do not assume that the goal of dialogue is agreement or that dialogue is of value only if it leads to agreement. I believe in dialogue as openhearted address and response. But I have no assumptions concerning its outcome. I do not even assume--how could I?--that there will always be genuine dialogue, even though both partners may truly desire it. We need to be face to face to talk, but that oppositeness all too often crystallizes into opposition that transforms genuine dialogue into debate or even violence.

Controversy for the Sake of Heaven

The only perspective from which we can find comfort in the face of such tragic conflict is the Talmudic approach that holds that "every controversy that takes place for the sake of heaven endures." "These and those are the words of the living God." This is completely contrary to Aristotelian logic with its assumption that a statement and its opposite cannot both be true. To say that both sides will endure does not mean that God will ultimately judge who is right and who is wrong. We each witness for our own "touchstone of reality" and confirm one another even while opposing the other. If the witness of the other is genuine, I believe that, except for the tragic realities of which I spoke above, it is always possible to respond and to move toward greater openness: I can open myself to what the other says; I can recognize the witness of the other even in opposing it; and I can reaffirm my own witness in dialogue with that of the other.

In her work counseling Cambodian refugees in Los Angeles, my friend Marsie Scharlatt encountered a situation that seems to me the very opposite of the dialogue of touchstones as an approach to interreligious dialogue. Because of the help that the missionaries gave to them, the Cambodian refugees thought it only right to let their children go to the missionary schools. The Cambodians, practically all of whom are Buddhist, discovered that their children were becoming Christian and no longer respected their parents or their parents' religion. Thanks to the intervention of Marsie and the other counselors, a community meeting was called between staff members and the local interfaith council. Faced with the consternation and grief of the parents, several of the missionaries agreed to stop their efforts to convert the children. But several others refused, saying it was their Christian duty to save the souls of these children no matter what the cost to the parents! This is the death of dialogue.

The Lived Meeting with Reality as Criterion of Truth

Our ultimate criterion of meaning and truth is not the proliferation of a religious creed but the lived new meeting with reality. To ask for criteria for the validity and truth of touchstones "more precise and practical" than this, as some do, is to hanker after a criteriological Archimedean point outside the dialogue. Useful as precision and definition are for the exact sciences, the true humanity and the very meaning of the dialogue of touchstones depends upon its being brought back to the fruitful disagreement of lived speech between persons whose meanings necessarily differ because of the difference of their attitudes, their situations, their points of view. Despite our differences and contradictions, it is necessary to continue talking and sharing, for this is the only direction in which we can hope to reach that genuine community to which this book points.

CHAPTER 14

CONCLUSION
Toward a Community of Communities

Restoring Relational Trust

There must be a restoration of relational trust for genuine community to acquire significant strength in our time and in the ages that follow. The restoration of relational trust is necessary not only for the one-on-one relationships of friendship, love, and marriage, as well as the family, but for every aspect of the community and society with which we have dealt and many more with which we have not.

One cannot legislate relational trust nor can one make it the goal of planned social action. Yet there are things that we can do at every level to help bring it about. One of these is the recognition of its centrality for therapy, education, family life, community, and the fellowship that holds society together. Another is the movement to build climates of trust insofar as the situation, the structure, and our resources allow.

Naturally a "climate of trust" too cannot be made into a specific goal without destroying the spontaneity and the "betweenness" that are essential to such a climate. Yet we can become more aware of what genuine listening and responding is. We can become more sensitive to the voices that are not ordinarily heard within the family, community, and society. We can overcome that mistrust founded on hysteria that imagines that something dreadful will happen if we allow such voices to express points of view that may not accord with our own or even with the leadership of the group. In all of these we are limited by the severe grace of the situation, for trust and trustworthiness are not ultimately personality characteristics that inhere *in* particular persons. They are realities of the "between," and the between cannot be willed or manipulated though we must work toward it as a general direction of movement.

The Movement toward a Community of Communities

True community cannot be a closed one. To continue to grow in the confirmation of otherness it must have its own ground and center, to be sure, but it must also be in open dialogue with individuals and communities outside itself. The search for the "blessed community" is ultimately an illusion, whether it expresses itself in the form of a community of affinity, or like-mindedness, a church or cult, or a commune that shuts itself off from the rest of society. The dialogue among genuine communities can only be sustained if there is a steady movement from casual and desultory contacts to regular, fruitful interaction and from there to what may be called the "community of communities."

The "community of communities" is a term I have taken from Martin Buber's classic study of utopian socialism, *Paths in Utopia*. What Buber offers in his conclusion to *Paths in Utopia* is a movement in the direction of fellowship and social spontaneity and a limitation of the dominance of the "political principle" of government to only what is necessary at any given time to preserve the unity of society. In his concluding chapter, "In the Midst of Crisis," Buber claims that the primary aspiration of all history is a genuine community of human beings. By *genuine* community he means *community all through,* a community based "on the actual and communal life of big and little groups living and working together, and on their mutual relationships." For such a communal life to exist, the collectivity into which the control of the means of production passes must facilitate and promote in its very structure and in all its institutions the genuine common life of the various groups composing it.

A community does not need to be "founded," Buber asserts. Wherever historical destiny has brought a group of people together in a common fold, a living togetherness, constantly renewing itself, can already be there, and all that needs strengthening is the immediacy of relationships. The communal spirit has always been able to overcome the danger of seclusion by breaking windows for itself so that it may look out onto people, mankind, and the world. But a community of communities does have to be built, and this can be done only if the process of community building runs all through the relations of the communities with one another. "A nation is a community to the degree that it is a community of communities."

Can True Communities Become a Community of Communities/

What might we possibly find meaningful today in Martin Buber's strange words that community must ever again miscarry and that this is the way that we must go. To the dreadful phenomenon of "psychologism" of which he spoke--seeing what happens between persons as actually manifestations of the individual psyche—we must add .fear of otherness, mistrust, self-involvement, mutual exploitation, categorization and fixing people in social roles, anxiety about disconfirmation, "seeming," and , perhaps above all, the tragedy of the limits of our resources that makes each of us what we are and that stands in the way of our turning conflict and contradiction into fruitful tension and meaningful dialogue.

A community of communities does not imply a decentralized as opposed to a state socialism, but a movement in the direction of fellowship and social spontaneity and the limitation of the domination of the "political principle." Such a community of communities would be based on the actual and communal life of big and little groups working together, and on their mutual relationships. This can only be done, to be sure, if the process of community building runs all through the relations of the communities with one another.. Of course, for this to take place on an international scale the worldwide barriers of communication that are caused by custom, language, nationality, traditional enmity, suspicion, and mutual mistrust would have to be overcome to a greater or lesser degree.

The community of communities is not, of course, any sort of panacea, technique, or blueprint! Yet *this* is the goal for which we must now strive if we are to have any hope of making headway in the task of overcoming the dreadful and truly terrible personal, interhuman, social, communal, and societal events that we are now facing.

Our very pointing to the ultimate goal of a community of communities brings us back to the general and specific barriers to the confirmation of otherness that we have discovered at every level. Once the community of communities is envisaged as a nation and still more as a community of nations, we must add to the limits we have already looked at, the worldwide barriers of communication that are caused by custom, language, nationality, traditional enmity, suspicion, and mutual mistrust. These limits are not so easily overcome as communications experts seem to expect. Even the advent of the age of the computer and simultaneous translation and instant worldwide transmission cannot in themselves overcome the interpersonal, international, and existential mistrust that dogs our every step. Yet these things *can* be used to move in that direction, as can television, travel, education, and a thousand other innovations that the ocean of progress has thrown up on our shores.

Community Must Ever Again Miscarry

Although Martin Buber never ceased to believe in the unfinished task of building genuine community, he also held that community in our time must ever again miscarry and that this miscarrying is itself a part of the way of community.

Why must community in our time ever again miscarry? One of the reasons is that given by Buber himself--the "dreadful psychologism" that leads us to convert the events that happen between us and other persons into some intrapsychic phenomenon. Other reasons are the general limits to the confirmation of others--fear of what is not like ourselves, mistrust, self-involvement, mutual exploitation, categorization and fixing people in social roles, and anxiety about being left out. Still other reasons can be found in the specific obstacles that arise at any given time in specific situations, as we encounter them in the field.

Tragedy and the Paradox of Confirmation

If the between cannot be willed or manipulated, then neither can the confirmation that results from genuine dialogue. This is another, deeper, reason why community must miscarry. The paradox of confirmation itself is that it is essential to human existence yet cannot be aimed at as a specific goal. We can neither will to confirm nor will to be confirmed; for confirmation is a reality of the between.

When we go from the consideration of the confirmation of the individual person in person-to-person relationships to the confirmation of otherness in community and society, we begin to glimpse tragedy in the deepest sense of the term. This is the tragedy of the limits of our resources, which make each of us what we are and which stand in the way of our turning conflict and contradiction into fruitful tension and meaningful dialogue. It is in light of these limitations that we must speak also of the limits of the confirmation of otherness and the destiny of communities in our time to miscarry.

Yet because confirmation of otherness is an affair of the between, then it is, in the existential meaning of the term, a "grace." There are two reasons we cannot will to confirm or to be confirmed. The first is that we cannot handle both sides of the dialogue. The second is that a dialogue is more than a sum of the two sides. It is a manifestation of the "between" that comes into being in that dialogue which we cannot control or apprehend.

The Hidden Confirmation in the Depths of History

If this is so, then the real confirmation of otherness is not identifiable with social and political effectiveness or with historical success. The latter may be thought of in terms of cause and effect, plan and execution, effort and victory. Confirmation of otherness cannot.

It is a reality that takes shape in the depths of history and retreats to those depths when it is obscured, manipulated, or overridden, as seems to be increasingly the case in the age we have now entered.

Outer history sees only success. Inner history knows that what is really effective is the way toward genuine community --the movement to the limits of the confirmation of otherness in any given situation and the acceptance of these often tragic limits. Genuine community is not an ideal but a direction of movement and one, moreover, that we must take if we are to move at all toward the restoration of relational trust. This is the mystery and grace of the "between" that resides in our midst in the depths of history.

A Different Philosophy of Action

This is a different philosophy of action, one that sees effectiveness not in political success but in the restoration of relational trust, in healing through meeting, in bringing the hidden human image out of its hiding, in creating genuine community. When Senator McGovern conceded defeat in the 1972 elections he quoted the verse from Deutero-Isaiah, "Those who wait upon the Lord shall run and not be weary, shall walk and not be faint" (*Isaiah* 40:31). Though this allusion to Deutero-Isaiah's "suffering servant" did not prevent McGovern from following Senator Eugene McCarthy into the oblivion of those candidates who do not get elected, it touched me deeply at the time.

After my book *The Hidden Human Image* was published in 1974, I was struck by how quickly some of its major concerns--from education and encounter groups to social witness and nonviolent action--seemed to go out of date. Suddenly few persons cared about these matters or about communes or any of the other breakthroughs of the '60's except for liberalized sex (in a time before the onslaught of the AIDS epidemic) and women's liberation.

What we have lived through in the years since 1974 is mind-boggling in the most exact sense of the term: the incredible blood bath of the Khmer Rouge in Cambodia; the rise of fundamentalism in Iran, Pakistan, and large parts of the Islamic world as well as, in different form, in America; the American backlash against every form of social welfare and the dismantling of the social welfare system; the eroding of the gains made in guaranteeing women the right of abortion; the civil war in Lebanon; the tearing down of the Berlin Wall and the liberation of the countries of Eastern Europe from the domination of the Soviet Union; the collapse of the Soviet Union itself; the end of the "cold war" and the beginnings of disarmament; the bloody civil war in what was Yugoslavia, the successful inroads into apartheid in South Africa, the liberation of Mandala and his election as President, the devastating war against Iraq for the liberation of Kuwait, the terrible trauma of 9/11, and now, sadly, the second war in Iraq, supposedly justified by the claim that Iraq had weapons of mass destruction and the claim that Sadam Hussein had links to Osama bin Laden, the architect of 0/11 (President Bush and Vice-President Cheyney have since admitted that both claims were in error), and most recently the gen9cide in Dafur.

What can we do in the face of all this? The answer is simple yet in practice infinitely complex. As far as our resources allow in each new situation we must move in the direction of restoring relational trust and creating, ever anew, genuine community and real partnership.

References

Aker, D. (1993). Renegades and realists: Three women for many nations, *Women's Times* (San Diego), April, 1993

Anzadúa, G. editor (1990). *Making Face, Making Soul, Haciendo Caras: Creative and Critical Perspectives by Women of Color.* San Francisco: An Aunt Lute Foundation Book.

Buber, M. (1958) *I and Thou*, 2nd rev. ed. with Postscript by Author Added. Trans by Ronald Gregor Smith. Chas. Scribner's, New York

Buber, M.(1958) *Paths in Utopia* Trans.. by R. F. C. Hull. Beacon Press, Boston.

Buber, M. (1985) *Between Man amd Man*, trtans. By R. G. Smith with an Introduction by Maurice Friedman. Macmillan, New York..

Buber, M. (1988) *The Knowledge of Man: A Philosophy of the Interhuman.* Ed. with an Introductory Essay (Chap. l) by Maurice Friedman, trans. by Maurice Friedman and R. G. Smith, Humanities Press International, Atlantic Highlands, NJ (now distributed as a Humanity Book by Prometheus Books, Amherst, New York).

Buber, M. (1983 & 2995) *A Land of Two Peoples: Martin Buber on Jews and Arabs.* Edited with Commentary and a new Preface by Paul Mendes-Flohr. University of Chicago Press Cjicago.

de Beauvoir, S. (1971). *The Second Sex.* Trans. & Ed. By H. M. Parshley. New York: Alfred A. Knopf.

Eisenstein, Z. (1994), *The Color of Gender: Reimaging Democracy* The University of California Press, Berkeley.

Eisenstein, Z. (1996). *Hatreds: Racialized and Sexualized Conflicts in the 21st Century.* Routledge, New York and London:

Friedman, Maurice[22])1072) *Touchstones of Reality: Existential Trust and the Community pf Peace E. P. Dutton, New Y ork.*

Friedman, Maurice (1974). *The Hidden Human Image.* Delacorte Press, New York.

Friedman, Maurice (1982, 1983, 1984). *Martin Buber's Life and Work: The Early Years—1878-1923*; *The Middle Years* (1923-1945); *The Later Years* (1945-1065) E. P. Dutton, New York.

Friedman, Maurice (1983). *The Confirmation of Otherness: In Family, Community, and Society.* Pilgrim Press, New York.

Friedman, Maurice (1991). *A Heart of Wisdom: Religion and Human Wholeness.* State University of New York Press. Albany, New York.

Friedman, Maurice (1996). Editor-in-Chief, *Martin Buber and the Human Sciences.* SUNY Press, Albany, New York.

Jordan, J. V., Kaplan, A. G., Miller, J. B., Stiver, I. P., Surrey, J. L. (1991). *Women's Growth in Connection: Writings from the Stone Center.* Guilford Press, London and New York.

Petchesky, R. (1990). *Abortion and Women's Choice: The State, Sexuality, and Reproductive Freedom*, rev. ed. Northeastern University Press, Boston.

Endnotes

1   Maurice Friedman, *Encounter on the Narrow Ridge: A Life of Martin Buber* (New York: Paragon House, 1991). The paperback edition was published in 1993. In 1993 and 1998 two separate Spanish translations were published in Buenos Aires, Argentina, in 1999 a German translation was published in Germany, and in 2000 a .Japanese translation was published in Japan.

1   Martin Buber, *Tales of the Hasidim* (New York: Schocken Books, 1991), Book One – *The Early Masters*, p. 277.

2   Cf. Maurice Friedman, *To Deny Our Nothingness: Contemporary Images of Man*, 3rd revised & enlarged edition (Chicago: The University of Chicago Press, 1978), pp. 326-330.

3   *Los Angeles Times,* May 13, 1999, pp. Al, A 18, A 19.

4   Drs. Maria and Willy daVenza Crespo, "If God gave us free will, philosophy gives us the ability to exercise free will: Socratic dialogue for inmates in the federal jail in downtown San Diego"--a paper presented at the Second ASPCP International Conference for Philosophical Practice, Purdue University Calumet, Ma y 1 8-20 2007 This paper will be a part of the book that will come out of this conference..

5   I have based what I have paraphrased and quoted here on Rev. Crespo's thesis proposal for his doctorate of ministry with Seabury Institute in Chicago, but I can guarantee what is here from my

own years of acquaintance with Wilfredo Crespo and my own visits to his prison where I have seen him at work.

6   Drs. Maria and Willy daVenza Crespo, "If God gave us free will, philosophy gives us the ability to exercise free will: Socratic dialogue for inmates in the federal jail in downtown San Diego"--a paper presented at the Second ASPCP International Conference for Philosophical Practice, Purdue University Calumet, Ma y 1 8-20 2007 This paper will be a part of the book that will come out of this conference..

7   I have based what I have paraphrased and quoted here on Rev. Crespo's thesis proposal for his doctorate of ministry with Seabury Institute in Chicago, but I can guarantee what is here from my own years of acquaintance with Wilfredo Crespo and my own visits to his prison where I have seen him at work.

8   Philip Lamy, *Millennium Rage: Survivalists, White Supremacists, and the Doomsday Prophecy* (New York: Plenum Press, 1996), p. 117.

9   Lamy's book gives a detailed and splendid history of this powerful trend within Christianity, linked to the very origins of Christianity and carried on throughout two thousand years. The movie actor Mel Gibson's own movie "The Passion of the Christ" is a currant example' I was not surprised by a recent report that when the inebriated Gibson was given a ticket by a police officer he made an openly anti-Smirticattack against the officer just in case he was Jewish!

10 *Ibid*, pp. 119, 128, 130, 132-134, 173, 260.

11 *Ibid.*, p. 266.

12 R.D. Laing, *Self and Others* (New York: Pelican Books, 1971, p.136)

13 R.D. Laing, *The Politics of Experience* (New York: Ballantine Books, 1967), p. 97.

14 On this aspect of the problematic of confirmation, see my discussion on Kafka in Maurice Friedman, *Problematic Rebel: Melville, Dostoievsky, Kafka, Camus,* 2nd rev. & radically reorganized ed. (Chicago: University of Chicago Press, 1970), pp. 374-399, 476-483.

15 *The Way of Life: According to Lao-tzu,* trans. by Witter Bynner, #67, p. 68 f

16 See Maurice Friedman, *The Healing Dialogue in Psychotherapy* (New York: Jason Aronson, 1985), Chap. 16: "The Problematic of Mutuality," pp. 169-194.

17 Martin Buber, *Between Man and Man,* trans. by R. G. Smith with an Introduction by Maurice Friedman (New York: Macmillan Co., 1985), "Dialogue," p. 7 f.

18 References to the famous economist Milton Friedman and to me get mixed up if only M. is provided in place of the first name. I even saw this happen once in the same article. Therefore, I hxve set down my full first name to avoid confusion..